GUILTY

...UNTIL PROVEN INNOCENT

Teachers and Accusations of Abuse

by Mathew D. Olson and Gregory Lawler

NEW
FORUMS
Stillwater, Oklahoma
U.S.A.

NEW FORUMS PRESS INC.

Published in the United States of America
by New Forums Press, Inc.
1018 S. Lewis St.
Stillwater, OK 74074
www.newforums.com

Library of Congress Cataloging-in-Publication Data

Olson, Mathew D.
 Guilty- until proven innocent : teachers and accusations of abuse / by
Mathew D. Olson and Gregory Lawler.— 1st American pbk. ed.
    p. cm.
 ISBN 1-58107-062-4 (alk. paper)
 1. School discipline—Law and legislation—United States. 2. False
testimony—United States. 3. High school teachers—Abuse of—United
States. 4. High school students—Abuse of—United States. I. Lawler,
Gregory J. II. Title.
 KF4159.O448 2003
 344.73'0793—dc21

                                                        2003006781

This book may be ordered in bulk quantities at a discount from New
Forums Press, Inc., P.O. Box 876, Stillwater, OK 74076 [Federal I.D.
No. 73-1123239]. Printed in the United States of America.

Cover design by Mac Crank.

To Vikki,
my life's teacher of
unconditional love.
M.D.O

To all my teachers
whose dedication
and support inspired
my professional life.
G.J.L.

Table of Contents

Section One – Legislative Cases

The Anderson case demonstrates the need for mandatory discipline for students who are proven to have made false allegations against educators.

The Ridgeway case highlights the need for accused teachers to have better access to school district's investigative records and the need to scrutinize the motives of administrators dealing with allegations of abuse.

The Chapel case deals with the impetus behind the creation of legislation to protect teachers who are accused of abuse for actions resulting from the responsible execution of their daily duties.

The Young case underscores the need for teachers to fight all unjust disciplinary actions before they become part of their personnel record.

The Marks case illustrates the need for severe mandatory repercussions for educators who make false allegations of abuse against other educators.

The Apple case was one of the first cases to test the Chapel legislation.

The Ericksen case examines the role that the "report anything that is uncomfortable" standard plays in the chilling of academic freedoms.

Section Two – Media Cases

Heisenberg's Uncertainty Principle, a physics theory, is taken out of its original context to explain how the media affects the perception and outcome of teacher abuse cases.

Acknowledgements

Writing a book is a process and every step of the way there was someone to lighten the burden. Thanks to Teri Slaymaker for her fine editorial skills and ability to push a cranky writer.

The authors would like to thank Sally Haines for her continuous and unwavering support, dedication and commitment to excellence.

This book could not have been written without the efforts of the Colorado Education Association. The authors particularly wish to thank CEA Executive Director Phil Moeckli, General Counsel Martha Houser, and attorneys Cathy Cooper, Sharyn Dreyer and Bradley Bartels, as well as the numerous employees who played roles in the cases examined.

Thanks to Kathleen Lyons, General Counsel Michael Simpson and the National Education Association for their advice and support.

Special thanks to first reader Karla Lane for her efforts to improve the quality of this work.

Thanks also to John Meyer for providing a different prospective on the material and for not counting my golf strokes.

Lastly, thank you to Victoria Olson for her faith, love and support throughout the entire process.

Note to the Reader

With but two exceptions, the authors of *Guilty Until Proven Innocent* have changed all names of individuals, places and other important identifying information in order to avoid revictimizing the teachers involved in the cases examined. Some conversations, interviews and testimonies have been condensed to facilitate flow.

Foreword

One aspect of my job as a defense attorney for the Colorado Education Association is to visit local schools and give the faculty a presentation on how to avoid becoming falsely accused of a crime. My last presentation was to a group of teachers at a high school in Denver, Colorado. To get into the school, I passed through as much security as that at Denver International Airport.

The changes in our schools have occurred rapidly. In the 1980's I was a student at Regis High School in Denver, Colorado. At that time, contraband was considered gum and comic books. As I passed through the metal detectors and had a wand run over the course of my body, the change in American schools was crystallized for me. The innocence of American youth is gone. It has been replaced by guns, knives, pipe bombs and drugs.

The security guards were polite and tried to limit my inconvenience, but I was frustrated by the delay. I watched as students, late for school, entered the building. The security measures seemed routine to them. It was simply their reality and they accepted metal detectors as part of their daily lives. As I observed the students, I couldn't help wonder – what had changed? I eventually realized that the answer to my question could be found in my daily work.

During my fifteen years with the CEA, I have defended about two thousand teachers accused of abuse against students. Of those cases, I'd estimate that almost ninety percent were false allegations. The accusations were usually made by students with an axe to grind. Usually the student had been disciplined by the accused teacher or had been given a failing grade. The accusation was the student's way of lashing out.

The simple fact is that disciplining students can lead to false allegations. Fearing a lawsuit by the parents of the accuser, school boards punish the teacher; they then limit the methods of discipline for other faculty members. As teachers' ability to discipline students has diminished, a direct correlation can be seen in the escalation of violence in schools. Students no longer fear the repercussions of their actions.

School boards aren't the only cause of the lessening ability for student discipline. Local legislators also play a key role. Some of the teachers I've defended have been guilty. Their crimes were heinous and made me sick to my stomach. Society views these teachers in much the same way. There is a deep revulsion for anyone who could harm a child. The natural instinct of our society is to protect our children. Thus, being a democratic society, politicians have introduced laws that limit teachers' protections. This is a case of a few bad teachers ruining the system for all the hard working, dedicated teachers out there.

Imagine yourself as a teacher. You see two students engaged in a fist fight. Your first instinct is to break up the fight. But instead of doing what you feel is right, you have to think through the consequences of your actions. If you grab a student, you can have abuse allegations leveled against you. If you stop the fight, a student can say that you hit him and show an administrator a bruise obtained in the fight; and you are facing termination. If you do nothing and a student gets severely hurt, you are civilly liable. It is truly a no-win situation.

One of the cases I document in *Guilty Until Proven Innocent* deals with such a situation. The teacher was brought up on dismissal charges, and the case eventually found its way to the appeals court. That teacher went on to draft legislation to protect teachers acting responsibly, but even that limited protection is not fullproof.

Laws are challenged in the courts, and the new law is no exception. In a perfect world, this would not be a problem. However, judges are not immune from society's feelings of revulsion. The laws that protect teachers are often changed or weakened in the courts. Judges have a broad power to rewrite the laws; and in the cases of teacher protections, the courts are inclined to limit the protections. In my experience, judges are willing to bend over backwards to allow school districts the freedom to discipline teachers as they please.

The pendulum has swung so far to the side of the school district that students have become aware of teachers' vulnerability. Teachers must fear retaliatory accusations and account for that possibility in their every action.

If I were an outsider looking in on the situation, I would expect this situation not to be a problem for veteran teachers. However, from my vantage point on the front line, I know that this is a misconception. The majority of my cases involve teachers with years of experience. The reason for this is so simple it's easy to overlook. Experience often leads to complacency; veteran teachers let their guard down. They aren't as careful as they should be. As a result, veteran teachers are often falsely accused of abuse.

The teaching profession is a profession under attack by legislators, students and society in general. As a member of the CEA, I am tasked with protecting the rights of all teachers. Co-authoring *Guilty Until Proven Innocent* is a means to that goal. I believe that an open dialogue in the public domain is necessary to facilitate a discussion about the rights of teachers. By examining some of my cases for the shortcomings of the law, I hope to illustrate the plight of teachers wrongly accused of crimes against students.

Through an open dialogue, it might be possible to move the pendulum back to neutral ground and allow teachers the means necessary to discipline students without the fear of prosecution. If teachers can discipline students, perhaps I won't have to walk through any more metal detectors.

- Gregory J. Lawler, esq.

Introduction

Background

The Salem Witch Trials ended more than three centuries ago, but the persecution of innocent citizens left a dark residue that still clings to the American conscience. It is especially apparent when teachers are falsely accused of crimes against students.

Modern allegations of abuse against children are viewed by today's society the same way the Puritans viewed accused witches. Short of death, there was no way to be sure the accused were innocent of all crimes.

No matter what evidence the accused brought forth, the stain of the allegation permanently tarnished the public's perception of them. In the days of the Salem Witch Trials, the accused faced ostracism locally. In the modern world, equipped with satellite television, the internet, fax machines and other technologies that provide instant communication, the reputation of the accused is often quickly and irreparably shattered nationwide.

Once a student makes an allegation against a teacher, the presumption of innocence – central to American jurisprudence – vanishes. The impetus of proof falls on the accused. Proof of innocence is held to a higher standard than the evidence needed to file criminal charges.

According to statistics kept by the Social Services Sex Offender Registry, the state of Colorado is among the national leaders for reports of teachers physically and sexually abusing students since 1986. The rise in reports of teachers abusing students coincides with the Colorado legislature's adoption of new guidelines for reporting abuse. The guidelines mandate that any reasonable suspicion of abuse must be reported to authorities. Thus, if a student alleges to an educator that a teacher struck him, that educator must report the allegation, even if he believes the allegation is false. The guidelines were written to protect students, but the result was a spike in teachers being falsely accused of abuse. Because the standard is vague and all encompassing, it has opened the door for retaliatory accusations against teachers. What was meant to be a shield is now a sword in the hands of a student who might resent disciplinary actions taken by a teacher.

The Colorado Court of Appeals and the Colorado Supreme Court are currently tasked with sorting through the language of the legislation and arriving at consistent standards for reporting allegations of abuse. However, courts are reluctant to apply stricter standards for fear of leaving students vulnerable to documented cases of abuse. While students and teachers wait for the courts to rule on accepted standards, students are asked to report allegations of abuse to school officials, even when they are not sure if the teacher's actions should be reported.

Students are confused as to what constitutes inappropriate touching; therefore, school districts are now required to teach students the proper legal method to make an allegation. Student reporting standards vary within the local school districts because state guidelines allow individual districts to implement their own policies.

School administrators are faced with the additional pressure of an increasingly litigious American society. Student allegations must be met with swift and severe action against the teacher to stave off legal action by parents, even if the resulting action violates a teacher's constitutional rights. Educators can and do fight for their rights, but juries and courts historically have not awarded damages for false allegations of abuse. The lack of awards is a direct result of parental testimony that their children reported the alleged abuse to them and they felt like they needed to act on the information.

Every state has a teacher's union dedicated to serving and protecting the interests and rights of educators. The Colorado Education Association (CEA) created a separate department to assist teachers in legal matters. The National Education Association

(NEA) is the national teachers' union. The NEA leaves reporting standards and policies to the individual unions. Because laws vary from state to state, the teachers unions run autonomously.

A teacher who has been accused of abuse faces multiple legal proceedings. If authorities believe there is enough evidence to warrant a criminal charge, the teacher faces a possible jail term. Even if the police decide not to press criminal charges, the teacher and the school district can face a civil suit brought by the parents of the alleged victim. Monetary damages can be awarded against the school district and the individual teacher. If no criminal charges are pressed or civil suit filed, the school can still bring termination charges against a teacher. The school district notifies the teacher in writing that it intends to dismiss the teacher. Then the process calls for a termination hearing. The hearing is presided over by a neutral hearing officer who makes a finding of facts and a recommendation to the school board. The board can still terminate the teacher even if the hearing officer recommends retention. Following the school board's actions, appeals can be filed in the state courts.

Prior to the high influx of teachers accused of abuse because of the Colorado legislative changes in 1986, the CEA did not have an in-house counsel assigned only for the purposes of criminal defense. The low number of cases prior to 1986 made such a position cost prohibitive. When the number of teachers accused of abuse escalated, the CEA encountered a problem with the continuity of the cases. The teachers who faced criminal, civil, license revocation and termination proceedings had three different attorneys, each with his own area of expertise. The first attorney to touch the case was generally an outside criminal defense counsel. The attorney's goal was to avoid jail time for the accused, and that attorney did not have the expertise to predict how their actions would affect the civil and termination proceedings that were still pending.

Teachers criminally charged have the most rights and protections because of the potential loss of freedom. Loss of money and career is determined by American courts to be less severe, and the rights of the accused in civil and termination proceedings diminish as a direct result of that belief. The burden of proof in the different legal arenas is vastly different. Criminal proceedings generally involve a jury and the standard is, beyond a reasonable doubt, the highest legal standard in American jurisprudence. Civil proceedings also are usually tried to a jury, but the standard of proof is by a preponderance of evidence or that it was more likely than not that the teacher was guilty. Termination hearings are tried to an impartial hearing officer who makes finding of facts and recommendations on retention to the local boards of education based on the civil standard. The boards of education have broad discretion to accept or reject the hearing officer's recommendation. License revocation proceedings are similar to the termination proceedings. The tactics and testimony a criminal defense attorney used in the criminal phase could actually be detrimental to the remaining proceedings.

Because of the differing burdens of proof, even if the accused teacher was found not guilty at the criminal and civil trial, a termination hearing often followed. The termination hearing then triggered several additional legal consequences. Despite the findings of the court system, a hearing to revoke the accused's teaching license immediately followed the termination hearing.

Following the resolution of the above proceedings, the teacher still had to endure the humiliation of having to remove his name from the social services' register as a child abuser.

The criminal case was a key component to all proceedings since the testimony, evidence or plea bargain used in the case guided the course of the remaining proceedings. The CEA became increasingly frustrated when their attorneys, representing teachers in the termination hearing and or civil suit, had to pick up a cold, lengthy trial transcript from the criminal case. Often, the embattled teachers could not afford adequate legal representation for the criminal proceeding and despite their innocence, accepted plea-bargains to lesser offenses. Very little could be done to save the teachers' careers in those instances, because a plea involves an admission of guilt.

The CEA's creation of an in-house counsel position mainstreamed the legal process for embattled teachers. As the problem continues to grow, the CEA is determined to expand their representation to district employees such as bus drivers and custodians as well as teachers. The CEA is only interested in protecting the rights of teachers who are unjustly accused, not actual abusers. If the CEA has credible evidence that a teacher is guilty, they actively work with school administrators to make sure incompetent or abusive teachers are removed from the classroom.

An Advocate Amid Adversaries

In 1986 the number of teachers accused of abuse in Colorado had escalated to the point that the CEA hired an in-house criminal defense counsel. One of the first attorneys CEA General Counsel Martha Houser interviewed was Greg Lawler.

As a law student at Denver University, Lawler had clerked for the CEA writing appellate briefs. After graduation, his one reliable source of income came from criminal defense cases the CEA had contracted out to him. Lawler was young and inexperienced, but Houser knew from her dealings with Lawler that he had the potential to be a good litigator.

Becoming an effective litigator is a learned skill. Talent and charisma help but to be effective, Lawler needed to experience the nuances of the courtroom that only years of trial work can provide. Law schools teach the law, but Lawler's early experiences at the CEA demonstrated to him that practicing it was a completely different proposition.

"In theory, the law is logical," Lawler said. "When you're in front of a jury, theory isn't always reality. Human emotions come into play. A good attorney needs to know the best way to present a case to a jury of his peers. It's possible for a defense attorney to follow every law perfectly and still lose at trial. A defense attorney also needs to know the legal nuances to even get his evidence heard. Sometimes, due to legal technicalities, an attorney needs to find a legal back door to get pieces of evidence or testimony into the record.

"An attorney learns to create the back doors by arguing cases in court. It's a skill that can't be taught in law school classrooms."

Despite Lawler's inexperience, he quickly realized the importance of his work.

"The one thing I brought to the CEA was the realization that Colorado teachers criminally charged needed an effective advocate," Lawler said. "I helped Marti [Houser] create the Criminal

Defense Program of the CEA. In every case I'd worked for them as a contractor, I saw the way society and the media treated the accused teachers. The teachers were at a great disadvantage by having separate lawyers for the different stages of their cases.

"By handling all of the teachers' legal needs, I hoped to balance out the legal process for them. The teachers needed someone to fight for their rights. My goal and the CEA's objective were the same. We not only wanted to defend the individual teacher, but we wanted to change the laws that thrust innocent teachers' careers into the legal system as well. The only way to make a difference was one case, one teacher, at a time."

Lawler realized that he was ill equipped to deal with the complications, difficulties and ramifications of a teacher facing allegations of abuse. Lawler sought help from the legal community and was fortunate to form a mentorship with Craig Truman, one of the most respected defense attorneys in the state of Colorado.

"Truman was a grizzled veteran," Lawler said. "He'd handled everything from high-profile murder cases to simple assaults. One variable in all of Truman's cases is his efforts to make sure the rights of the accused are not trampled by the justice system. Truman comes from a family of educators. So he was empathetic to the plight of teachers falsely accused. He wanted to fight for the underdog.

"Truman was and is a prominent attorney; I didn't think he'd return my calls. I was this green kid calling a man who has tried numerous high profile cases. Not many people in his position would have spoken to me. But he was interested in my work because of the legal issues and ramifications the teachers faced. When I laid out the facts of my first case, he identified with the teacher's plight and we immediately hit it off. We litigated that first case together in 1988 and won. After the trial, Truman told me to call him for help when I needed it. I only call him when a case has been tough because his time is so valuable. After each case we've tried together, I've learned lessons that apply to all of my cases. Our relationship has changed from a mentorship to a friendship over the years. I still call him for advice, though. I'm always looking to improve as an attorney and as a person."

Along with the lessons from Truman, Lawler also draws from

his own experiences for motivation. A product of a strict Jesuit up-bringing, Lawler has observed the vast changes in society's attitude towards disciplining students. According to Lawler, classroom discipline has gone from corporal punishment to politically correct behavior.

"Physical discipline wasn't abuse when I was growing up," Lawler said. "I was a wild child. My parents paid good money to send me to Catholic school with the expectation I would be physically disciplined. By physical discipline, I don't mean abuse. I mean disciplinary measures necessary to make me aware of societal norms and values, boundaries if you will. Making students aware of boundaries makes them better citizens. It's odd to say, but I think the physical discipline I experienced was done in a loving manner."

Lawler goes on to describe a priest who taught at his high school, who happened to be a former Golden Gloves champion and the Dean of Students responsible for discipline, who dragged unruly students to the gym for a round of boxing. The mischievous students usually ended up smarting. Lawler took his share of poundings. Despite the numerous rounds with the priest, Lawler was glad the priest didn't call home. The consequences would have been more than the priest could have administered.

"Times have changed. Growing up, if a teacher called home, my punishment was worse than even the priest could have given me. Today, parents feel guilty when their child is disrespectful. They think the student's actions are a result of their absence. That thought is painful for parents. Instead of dealing with the pain and disciplining their child, some parents look for a scapegoat to assuage their guilt. The person they blame is the teacher. Students know their parents are more apt to blame the teacher for their actions than discipline them. A teacher threatens to call home, and the student says, 'Go for it.' Most families have two working parents to pay the bills, and the parents are so drained when they get home, they don't have the time or energy to deal with unruly behavior. The Columbine tragedy couldn't have happened with my parents. They knew everything that was going on with me. I couldn't have stored one propane tank, let alone fifty, in the garage without my father asking for a damn good explanation."

Lawler realizes some of the teachers he defends have crossed the line, but he believes the vast majority of them are falsely accused. He partially faults the laws of the state for allowing the persecution of innocent teachers.

Guilty Until Proven Innocent examines several cases that directly affected Colorado laws. Cases, such as Joanna Chapel's, affected Colorado law. Chapel was a 98-pound female teacher who broke up a fight between two large, teenage boys. One of the boys was incensed that she stopped the fight. He accused her of abuse, stating the diminutive teacher caused a bruise he received in the fight. Despite the questionable nature of the charges, she was suspended. Lawler fought for her re-instatement and in the process helped change the law to protect teachers from accusations of abuse that arise from their daily responsibilities.

"The Chapel Legislation affects numerous cases in Colorado and nationally," Lawler said. "Following the enactment of the Chapel Legislation, other states adopted similar legislation. The new law was a valuable tool in stemming the tide of legislative efforts to strip teachers of their ability to defend against charges that arise from their normal duties. That protection is a cornerstone around which additional legislation can be built. If a teacher commits a crime, they deserve to be punished. The Chapel Legislation helps ensure innocent teachers aren't lumped in with the bad apples."

The Janet Young case was one of the first teacher abuse cases to test the new law. Young tapped a student on the head when the student dozed off during a lecture and was dismissed for abuse. The Young case eventually reached the Colorado Supreme Court on an appeal partially based on the new legislation.

Kurt Apple's case was the second case to reach the Colorado Court of Appeals under the Chapel Legislation. Apple was a second-year Denver Public Schools elementary school teacher, with a reputation for being a disciplinarian. When a girl, excited by a coming school party, refused to put the front legs of her chair on the ground, Apple pushed down on the chair to put all four legs on the ground. The girl reacted by leaning back, knocking the chair off balance. The girl fell to the floor and hurt her arm.

Apple was suspended and charged with abuse. The district court found Apple was immune from prosecution under the Chapel

Legislation. Despite the dismissal of charges, the Denver Public School's board opted not to renew his contract. Apple appealed the school board's decision to the Colorado Court of Appeals, where a termination hearing was granted. Apple was re-instated and continues to teach.

One of the legislative safeguards that Lawler and the CEA hope to see enacted is changes to the law to create mandatory repercussions for false allegations. Lawler believes the Joseph Anderson case would not have occurred if the proposed changes had been made prior to charges being filed against the teacher.

Anderson was a nationally acclaimed PE teacher. During a time of friction with his new principal, Anderson was suspended after he was accused of fondling three girls. All three victims' testimony proved to be blatantly false at trial. It was later proven that the girls fabricated their stories to retaliate for being made to run laps. Anderson's career was destroyed, but the conspirators were never punished.

"If a student lies and their story results in a teacher's dismissal, the student needs to face suspension," Lawler said. "As the law is applied now, students who fabricate allegations are not even held liable in a civil court. If there were mandatory consequences associated with lying, I believe many of the cases I deal with would not occur. Just because the law is written to protect minors from abuse, it should not mean that the students are immune from abusing the teacher, which is essentially what false allegations do."

Lawler maintains that along with greater accountability for students, there has to be increased scrutiny for the motives of administrators. Lawler asserts that the tension between Anderson and his principal contributed to the false allegations.

According to Lawler, the Lisa Ridgeway case is another example of friction between administrators and teachers giving rise to false allegations.

Lisa Ridgeway, a special education teacher, was terminated after three male students accused her of sexual misconduct. During the trial, it was revealed that the principal's handling of the accusation was swayed by his personal disdain for Ridgeway because of the principal's bias against overweight women. A hearing officer concluded that Ridgeway had done nothing illegal or immoral. Although she was exonerated, it took two years for Ridgeway to clear her name.

All of Lawler's cases highlight legislative deficiencies. One common deficiency involves the sharing of the schools' initial investigation records. Under Colorado law, a school's investigation records do not have to be provided to the defense before trial. Lawler states that numerous cases would not see the inside of a courtroom if that legal technicality were changed. Lawler points to the case of Robert Colin as an example.

Colin was a respected and decorated teacher before he was accused of sexual misconduct by two of his students, whom he had disciplined. Due to the girls' popularity, they were able to convince other female students to make similar allegations. When a county psychologist interviewed the students, during the school's investigation, all but one of the students recanted and admitted that their allegations were false. The prosecutor on the case ignored the new information and attempted to proceed to trial. Lawler, with the help of Truman, arranged a pretrial meeting with the District Attorney, who agreed to hear evidence, off the record. Following the meeting, the District Attorney dismissed all charges.

"We didn't have access to the psychologist's records until after the charges were filed," Lawler said. "If we had been given access to the records before charges were filed, the case wouldn't have progressed as far as it did. Once charges are filed and they become public, it's hard to undo the damage done. When a prosecutor's political aspirations are factored into the equation, the events building momentum to a trial become impossible to stop. Too many outside forces are pushing the case to a conclusion that may not be warranted. The meeting with the District Attorney was unusual, and it corrected the error, but it would not have been necessary if the law was changed. During an investigation, the teacher is a forgotten source of information. If the teacher was allowed to talk to investigators, with their counsel present, fabricated charges could be screened out. Until 1993, there was a law that stated a teacher was immune from criminal liability if they used reasonable force in the scope and course of their employment. I used that motion in all child abuse cases to get an initial screening hearing.

If the teacher acted reasonably, the court dismissed the charges. Every case I had that went through the screening process was dismissed. Now, the courts uniformly reject that motion, leaving that determination to the jury. There is no screening process for abuse cases anymore. It's easier now for false allegations to go to trial."

Part of the screening process Lawler feels is needed is input from the teacher.

"The investigative process needs to be collaborative between the schools, law enforcement officers and the teacher," Lawler said. "In most cases, the teacher is never granted a chance to give his or her side of the story. If the teacher's story is reasonable and credible, it exposes the fraudulent nature of the allegations. There are times the best course of action is for the teacher to remain silent. However, the teacher and their attorney should be allowed to make that determination."

Media Coverage and Controversy

Some cases are noteworthy because of the attention and treatment the media gave the cases. Most of the cases detailed involve innocent teachers accused of salacious crimes that fed the media's imagination and appetite. Cases with no merit were blown into front-page stories that were carried nationwide.

All of the media cases covered in *Guilty Until Proven Innocent* involved print stories that painted grim pictures of the accused teachers. The stories used inflammatory phrases to describe the accused and their crimes.

The English language is filled with words that conjure strong emotions. Whether unconsciously or purposefully, those words routinely find their way into the news stories of abused students. Small but powerful, these words lead to a public outcry that practically forces the districts to take action against the teachers involved. In several cases documented in this book, the district admitted they had little or no evidence to terminate the teacher involved but had to dismiss the educator because of the intense public pressure created by a blitz of negative publicity.

The media pressure on the cases examined is explained in a chapter called The Uncertainty Principle. The Uncertainty Principle is a theory of physics that states a person cannot take measure of a situation without affecting it. This theory is taken out of its original context and applied to high profile teacher abuse cases. Following *Chapter 8: The Uncertainty Principle*, Lawler's cases that received the most publicity are detailed.

The Darren Carr case is the first case examined. The case received regional media coverage that led to the teacher's dismissal.

Carr adopted the town prostitute's son, who was his student at the time. When the mother relinquished her rights to the child, she did not realize her state aid would be affected. When her welfare checks were reduced, she manufactured charges of sexual abuse, hoping to regain custody. The media portrayed Carr as a pedophile, despite his honorable intentions. After being cleared of all charges, he was still dismissed for having too close a relationship with a student. In their letter of dismissal, the school board cited negative publicity as a factor in their decision.

Before the Columbine massacre, the high school achieved a level of notoriety when the Al Wilder case drew national attention. Wilder had his senior Logic and Debate class view Bernardo Bertolucci's historical film *1900*. The film depicts a love story set amid the political turmoil of pre-WWI Italy. After hearing about the viewing of the movie, the principal used Columbine High School's media room to splice together scenes containing opiate use, violence, nudity and sexually suggestive images contained in the film into a three-minute video presentation. He showed his edited version of *1900* to the school board claiming the teacher had shown a pornographic movie to students.

Board members immediately recommended the dismissal of Wilder. Lawler fought to have Wilder re-instated, using many arguments; chief among them was that the students were old enough to rent the video themselves. There was also an assertion of Wilder's First Amendment right. The media soon carried the case nationwide and a national discussion of the case ensued. The media storm reached the ears of Bertolucci, who testified in the case.

An eventual finding by the Colorado Court of Appeals ruled that the principal created the only pornographic material in the case, and Wilder had reasonably used the film as a teaching aid. The case has grown in importance since the ruling because it occurred at Columbine High School, several years before the massacre by Dylan Klebold and Eric Harris.

The case highlighted the tensions between staff and administrators that caused erosion of communication. A finding by the Colorado Legislature's query into the Columbine slayings cited a lack of communication between teachers and their administrators as one reason Harris and Klebold's warning signs went undetected. That erosion of trust and communication is a central theme to almost every case examined in *Guilty Until Proven Innocent*.

Lori Salmon experienced the power of the media. Because of negative media coverage, Salmon nearly lost her job when she placed a child in a side room due to the student's disruptive behavior during class. The student made a complaint to the school's administrator and, after media publicity, the school district attempted to terminate Salmon. Prior to the hearing, Lawler was able to negotiate a deal with the school district to allow Salmon to keep her job.

The final media case is the Scott Rowland case. Rowland stopped a gang member from beating a boy into unconsciousness. To stop the beating, Rowland had to throw a basketball at the gang member, and he was charged with abuse.

Unlike other cases, Rowland's trial and subsequent acquittal were not covered by the media.

Two years after the incident, Rowland opened a newspaper to read that the gang member had beaten a cab driver to death. The media extensively covered the case against the gang member. Newspaper editorials asked why the gang members escalating violence was not stopped before it escalated to murder. Rowland believes that the school district and the media missed an opportunity to stop the violence with the school beating.

A Time for Change

All of the cases examined expose fundamental flaws in the legal and educational systems. Every case also highlights a growing tension between administrators and teachers. Today's students are aware of that tension and can use it to their advantage when a teacher falls out of favor with students.

"A chasm exists between principals and teachers on the front line of America's fight for its future," Lawler said. "Students who don't like a teacher, for any reason, can fabricate a charge and expect the teacher's dismissal."

Lawler goes on to explain that students' parents contribute to the problem.

"It used to be that if a parent had a complaint, he called the school. Now he calls a lawyer first. Principals are aware of this, so any allegation made is taken seriously. The student is believed. Schools are so aware of their liability, they forget the teacher is a human being endowed with inalienable rights," Lawler said.

According to Lawler, one source of the prevalent mistrust between teachers and administrators is the district's inability or unwillingness to support teachers with consistent student discipline. Teachers often see their disciplinary needs being disregarded by administrators who are conscious of standardized test scores. If a student misses classroom time due to disciplinary action, they often score lower on the tests, which determine state and federal funding.

Educators are encouraged to teach for the tests and discouraged from trying new and innovative ideas that may not translate into higher scores immediately. This increases the friction between administrators and teachers.

The gap continues to widen when school politics are added to the complicated equation. People cannot, by their nature, agree on everything. Because teachers bring their own experiences and personalities to the classroom, they do not always agree with the path that their superiors want them to take. Teachers who disagree do so at their own risk.

Both students and administrators easily single out outspoken teachers. A natural tension exists that can be exploited by those who wish to do so. Conversely, teachers who lack a strong presence and become administrative distractions are also vulnerable. Allegations of abuse terminate careers, regardless of the teacher's stature.

"Principals sometimes use abuse allegations as a way to get rid of a teacher they may have had a conflict with. Allegations of molestation or abuse are often the only way for administrators to terminate a non-probationary teacher. A criminal conviction is an automatic revocation of a teaching license. Too often, I think administrators blow allegations out of proportion for their own gain," Lawler said.

According to statistics the NEA has compiled, abuse is a problem in schools across the nation. Innocent teachers need protection from the same social pressures that led to the deaths of many Quaker women and men at the hands of the misguided Puritans. The Puritans' intent was not evil. Their unchecked power resulted in the persecution of innocents.

Teachers are increasingly under fire from both students and administrators. Legislative safeguards need to be enacted to protect teachers from unjust attacks. Citing numerous Colorado cases, this book examines the Chapel Legislation and its effect on teacher abuse cases and outlines changes to state and national laws that are still necessary. Statute changes lobbied for by the NEA and legislative changes currently under consideration in the Colorado House of Representatives, will be examined in depth, as well as proposed national legislation that adversely affects teachers.

The Salem Witch Trials ended only when ordinary citizens took charge and forced its end. By ignoring the problem of falsely accused teachers and sweeping it under the rug, a thick malaise has built up in the soul of American society. By illuminating the problem, it's possible to finally enact and enforce the laws that will leave our students, teachers and schools clean, safe and revitalized.

Lawler's cases provide a modern-day example of a system out of control but ultimately repairable.

"I believe the system can work," says Lawler. *"Guilty Until Proven Innocent* demonstrates that there are fundamental flaws. But as a reporter friend once told me, 'If you complain, you better have a solution.' I don't have all the answers. However, I do believe that through a thoughtful examination and dialogue, our society can reach a consensus on how best to protect both students and teachers. We all have a vested interest in seeing things put right."

Chapter 1
Joseph Anderson

The Beginning

The gymnasium at Pike's Peak Middle School was home to Joseph Anderson. Anderson originally attended Pike's Peak as a student. In 1984, after graduating from college with a degree in Physical Education, he sent Colorado Springs District 13 his only application for employment. Anderson was hired as a PE teacher at Pike's Peak. He wanted to devote his career to the school and its students.

Anderson toured the school on his first day of work. While walking through the classrooms he experienced a sense of deja vu. His memories were faint, but the classrooms seemed familiar. Anderson's last stop was his most anticipated – the gymnasium. As he surveyed its current condition, Anderson tried to remember how it had looked when he was a student, less than a decade before. Anderson envisioned sparkling floors, freshly painted walls, and racks of new equipment. The gym, like his memories, had faded.

The building had decayed quickly. The walls of the building were cracked, and the wood floor creaked with every step. The equipment the students used was in an equal state of disrepair. Anderson actually recognized some of the basketballs and archery equipment from his days as a student.

Anderson's first task after being hired was to modernize the gym and update the equipment. He personally designed modifications for the gym and applied to the district for the funds to remodel it. He was pleased when the request was granted. Within two years, the Pike's Peak gym was the envy of every middle school in the nation.

Anderson cared about his students and wanted them to embrace the lifestyle of physical fitness, just as he had done when he was a teenager. He was concerned about the growing national population of overweight students and saw gym class as a means of teaching students how to lead happy and healthy lives.

The curriculum hadn't changed much since his days as a student, and Anderson thought modern students needed a modernized program. Anderson developed new curriculum that included new methods of teaching and diversified activities. Anderson believed changes were needed, but some traditions needed to be maintained. Anderson believed in discipline. If you broke one of his class rules, you ran laps.

Like the remodeled gym, Anderson's innovations were respected and mimicked nationwide. As a result, Anderson was routinely asked to lecture at teachers' conferences and colleges nationally.

Anderson believed physical fitness skills learned in youth laid a foundation for a healthy lifestyle as an adult. Sociological studies Anderson read in college cemented his belief that students who participated in youth sports were less likely to get into criminal trouble or become obese adults.

Anderson volunteered to coach his middle school's basketball and track and field teams. As a teacher and a coach, he emphasized student participation and enjoyment. He didn't worry about the outcome of the games because he was focused more on the long-term benefits of participation.

Despite his later legal trouble, Anderson still looks back on his first fourteen years of teaching and coaching with pride. Beginning with the hiring of Principal Max Danser in 1998, Anderson's recollections became painful.

Changes and Friction

During his first fourteen years of teaching, Anderson had a mutual respect with then principal, Tim Barber. Barber retired at the end of the 1997 school year, and Max Danser was hired to replace him. Anderson hoped to foster the same relationship that he'd enjoyed with Barber, but Danser and Anderson were opposites in every respect.

Pike's Peak was Danser's third school in six years. Danser had moved out of his previous two schools in part because of conflicts with teachers over his strong anti-union stance. Danser alienated faculty members by rating members of the teacher's union lower in their personnel evaluations than non-union members. Danser was highly critical of the CEA and never missed a chance to voice his anti-union views.

Sexual harassment allegations had been made against Danser at his previous school, but charges were not filed. Prior to the allegation, the school board of the previous school had received numerous complaints about Danser from teachers and parents. Faced with mounting discontent by teachers and superiors, Danser chose to resign.

Anderson and Danser were quickly at odds. Danser regarded gym class as a waste of district money. He immediately began trimming the program's budget. Anderson took the budget cuts personally because the gym and its programs were like his children.

Anderson routinely challenged Danser at staff meetings. The two men would argue with their voices raised until the meeting finally had to be adjourned.

Another source of friction between the men was Anderson's pro-union stance. Anderson took every opportunity to pitch the union to his fellow teachers. Court documents revealed that Danser was aware of Anderson's views. He had often complained about Anderson's activism to fellow administrators, including Assistant Principal Sherry Turtle.

"The work environment in which Anderson taught was extremely hostile," Lawler said. "My client was aware of the animosity Danser felt for him and needed to be cautious. Danser was looking for a reason to oust him. Unfortunately, Anderson didn't heed the warning signs and walked into a bear trap."

In 1998, during a track meet, Anderson rubbed a girl's cramping calf muscle. He'd done the same thing numerous times to help both female and male students. This time, Anderson made a mistake. While rubbing a knot out of the calf, he made a remark to the student about how soft her skin was. The girl was bothered by the remark and told Principal Danser.

Despite numerous options of how to deal with the incident,

such as talking to Anderson, Danser placed a written reprimand, the first step towards termination, in Anderson's personnel file. He also stripped Anderson of all coaching duties. Anderson was angered by the severe disciplinary action and filed a grievance with the district.

Prior to Anderson's reprimand, a female teacher at Pike's Peak filed a sexual harassment lawsuit against Principal Danser. Anderson supported the teacher by giving a sworn statement to plaintiff's counsel. The lawsuit was eventually resolved out of court.

"The fact the sexual harassment suit occurred before the written reprimand against Anderson was fishy," Lawler said. "I felt that Danser's actions were purely retaliatory."

Anderson's professional life settled down for a few months. He continued teaching the same way he had for fourteen years. As a teacher, Anderson tried to be accessible to students. Any student with a crisis was able to talk with him and receive guidance. Anderson cared for his students, but he was also strict. In 1998, his discipline of several female students gave rise to the allegations that would destroy his career.

The Allegations

During his years of teaching experience, Anderson realized female students, more often than males, disliked physical education classes. He'd heard almost every excuse to be dismissed from participation. When those students were forced to attend, they did so reluctantly.

During a flag football class, Anderson observed three girls standing and watching the other students play. Terri Garner, Lisa Ruff, and Vanessa Wright were perpetual problems. He instructed the girls to begin playing. When they refused, he ordered the girls to run laps.

According to court documents, the girls went to Counselor Linda Allen's office immediately after class. They told Allen they didn't like Anderson and didn't want to go to class. Allen asked the girls why they didn't like Anderson, and they told her he was too strict. Allen sent the girls back to class.

The girls were back in her office again a week later. This time they claimed Anderson was pushing them to the point they feared injury. Allen realized the girls were still trying to find a way out of gym class and turned them away.

Another week went by. Garner, Ruff and Wright came back again. This time they complained Anderson was focusing on male students and neglecting the females of the class. Allen was frustrated. She told the girls not to come back unless they had a very good reason not to go to class.

The three girls came back to Allen's office a week later for the fourth and final time. This time they had a complaint Allen couldn't ignore. The girls claimed Anderson had touched their breasts. Allen didn't believe the girls' stories. But, due to district policy and state law, she had to report the allegations. She notified Assistant Principal Turtle, who then informed Principal Danser. Allen later testified that Danser took immediate action, despite the context of the complaints.

Danser summoned Anderson to his office and placed him on suspension, pending an investigation of the charges.

Before notifying the police, Danser called Garner, Ruff and Wright to his office. He told the girls he needed a written statement of every incident and the names of any witnesses. When the girls gave Danser a list of names, he summoned those girls to his office.

Danser placed all of the girls on the witness list, along with Garner, Ruff and Wright, in a room next to his office. He told them to write down everything they could remember about the events. He closed the door and left them unsupervised.

Secretaries, present in the office at the time, later told Lawler that they heard the three accusing girls coaching the witnesses on what to write. The secretaries were concerned that the girls were fabricating their stories and reported the incident to Danser. Danser disregarded their concerns.

After he had all of the written statements, Danser reported the allegations to the Colorado Springs sheriff's office. Deputy Joel Hernandez responded to the call. Hernandez began an investigation by talking to Garner, Ruff and Wright.

The girls briefly told the officers that Anderson had touched their breasts. Before they could give a detailed account, Danser handed the officer the written statements.

Next, Hernandez interviewed Danser. Danser explained how the allegations had come to his attention. Hernandez asked the principal for his assessment of Anderson. Danser claimed Anderson was a sub-par teacher who had problems with alcohol and gambling. Danser said he wasn't surprised by the allegations because they fit with Anderson's character.

The girls' statements and Danser's characterization of Anderson led Hernandez to believe an assault had occurred. The sheriff's office opened an official investigation the next day.

While the sheriff's office investigated the complaints, the girls' stories grew with each police interview. They were now claiming Anderson groped them on an archery range.

Garner, Ruff and Wright, as well as several additional female students, further alleged that Anderson would walk into the women's locker room while they were in various stages of undress. In November 1998, Anderson was charged with twelve counts of sexual assault.

Lawler's Investigation

After his suspension, Anderson's first call was to the CEA. Greg Lawler took the case. Lawler called Craig Truman for help. Lawler and Truman hired an investigator to begin examining the girls' stories. Lawler was suspicious because all of the alleged victim's statements matched each other word for word.

"Humans perceive things differently," Lawler said. "A Harvard Law professor once had his students watch a videotaped basketball game. He asked the members of the class to count how many times the basketball was passed. During the half-time intermission, a man in a gorilla suit ran onto the court. After the class viewed the game, the professor asked his students to describe the gorilla. The majority of them asked, 'What gorilla?'

"It was highly unlikely all of the students' stories would be that similar to each other's. I suspected that even though I was dealing with pre-teen girls, they had the intellect to orchestrate a conspiracy," Lawler said.

During his initial conversations with Anderson, Lawler realized why Danser was pushing so hard for criminal charges. There was a deep animosity between the two men and Danser wanted Anderson dismissed. Without a criminal conviction, the school district would face a lengthy, expensive and potentially embarrassing termination hearing, but a conviction on sexual assault was grounds for an automatic termination under Colorado State Law.

"I believe Danser wanted the state to do his dirty work," Lawler explained. "If Anderson was convicted, the district would also save close to fifty thousand dollars – the cost of a termination hearing."

Within the school district, Anderson's reputation was crushed. Lawler was surprised that the damage hadn't been more wide spread. For reasons Lawler cannot explain, there was no media coverage of the case.

"It might have been that the district knew they were wrong," Lawler said. "Or it may have been that the school district wasn't very good at public relations. Either way, my client caught a break."

The Trial

Without much fanfare, Anderson went on trial in January, 1999.

"The state's witness order was a little bizarre. They opened with the investigating officer, which is standard. But, in most cases I've tried, the principal is the second witness called," Lawler said. "Principal Danser never took the stand at trial. Instead, their second witness was Assistant Principal Turtle.

"I also assumed the state would call the counselor who first reported the allegations. Counselor Allen did not testify for the prosecution. When we got the state's witness list, we wondered why she wasn't listed, so I telephoned her. Allen told me she believed the girls were lying. She was the first witness I called when we were able to present our defense."

The alleging students did not testify until the second day of trial. Terri Garner took the stand and testified that Anderson put his arm over her shoulder and grabbed her breast while she was on the archery range. Garner testified in detail about where she was standing in relation to the target and how many times her arrows found the mark. She testified she blacked out after he grabbed her breast, but that she hadn't shot an arrow while Anderson was molesting her.

Lawler cross-examined Garner. He began by giving Garner a bow from the class. Lawler asked her to pull the string back. Garner tried, but couldn't.

"You had an arrow already strung and ready to shoot when Mr. Anderson grabbed your breast?" Lawler asked the girl.

"Yes. But I didn't shoot," Garner answered. "I was too stunned."

"How could you hold the string back for that long without help? You can barely pull the string back now?"

Garner couldn't answer.

"It's because Mr. Anderson was holding your hands steady and helping you pull the string back, isn't it?"

"Yes, that's right."

"If he had one hand holding the bow steady and one helping you pull the string back, how did he touch your breast?"

Garner couldn't explain.

Next, Lawler questioned Garner about statements she made to Micah Rasner, the investigator for the District Attorney's office. Garner had given Lawler's investigator a contradictory statement.

"Did you tell Ms. Rasner that Mr. Anderson would come up to you and put his arm around you and that sometimes he'd touch your breast area?" Lawler asked.

"I did not," Garner answered.

"If Ms. Rasner wrote that in her report, she would be wrong?"

"She would," Garner answered.

"You also told my investigator that Mr. Anderson came into the woman's locker room over forty times. In Ms. Rasner's report, she states you told her it was only twice. Which is correct?"

"I could only remember two times when I talked to her. Now I remember more."

"When did you remember more?"

"Later on," Garner answered.

"After you talked to your friends?" Lawler asked.

"That would be right."

After Garner's testimony, the trial was recessed for the day. In the hallway of the courthouse, the prosecutor approached Lawler and Truman.

"He saw his case was falling apart and offered us a plea," Lawler said. "The reduced charge he offered was a simple misdemeanor. Anderson was tempted to take it. It would've spared my client from further humiliation. Anderson was showing some wear and tear from the whole deal. He hadn't been sleeping very much. We told the DA we would accept, provided the school agreed to no disciplinary action."

The DA arranged for a meeting between Anderson's attorneys and the school district's representatives. After an exhaustive second day in court in which many of the alleged witnesses testified, Lawler, Truman and Anderson made their way to the school district's administration building. The prosecutor greeted Lawler's group and led them to a room. He told them the school district's representatives would be in soon.

In the next room, Lawler could see Danser, the school district's attorney and the prosecutor talking. Two hours later, Danser and the district's attorney walked out of the building without saying a word to Lawler, Truman or Anderson.

"After they left, the prosecutor came to us. He was a little red-faced. After he explained that the district had refused to even discuss a plea, he apologized for making us wait. I accepted his apology. The school district never apologized, but that was fine with me. I figured they'd get a nice helping of crow in court," Lawler said.

When the trial resumed, the prosecutor called Lisa Ruff to the stand. Ruff testified she had been groped on the archery range and that she had seen Anderson walk through the locker room while she was dressing. Ruff also alleged Anderson had gone through her possessions without her permission.

Truman cross-examined Ruff. Truman used the same tactics he had with Garner. Ruff had the same difficulties explaining the archery range that Garner did, but claimed she was telling the truth about her other allegations.

Truman asked Ruff to describe the circumstances in which she had seen Anderson walk through the girls' locker room.

"I was getting my backpack out of my locker and I felt someone pass behind me," Ruff said.

"If your back was to the person, how did you know it was Mr. Anderson?"

"Because Terri Garner saw him and told me later."

"You mentioned seeing Mr. Anderson go through your backpack. Do you know why he was doing that?"

"Probably looking for underwear."

"There are no assigned lockers, correct?"

"Yes. We use it for the class period only."

"Then how did Mr. Anderson know the backpack was yours?"

"He didn't. He probably didn't care," Ruff said.

"Isn't there a policy against leaving possessions in a locker once class is over?"

"Yes," Ruff answered.

"So if Mr. Anderson found your backpack, wouldn't it make sense that he look in it. He needed to find out whose it was so he could give it back to its owner?"

"Yes."

"And Mr. Anderson gave it back to you. Didn't he?"

"Yes, the next day."

"So, then there was nothing inappropriate about his behavior?" Truman asked.

"Not really. No," Ruff answered.

Vanessa Wright took the stand next. She testified she had witnessed the incidents on the archery range and had seen Anderson walk through the locker room. This time, Lawler handled the cross-examination.

Lawler asked Wright to explain where she was standing on the archery range when her friends were allegedly groped.

"I'm not sure," Wright answered.

"You weren't standing in front of Ms. Garner. After all, she had a bow and arrow ready to fire. Can we agree you were either standing on her left or right side?"

Wright agreed with Lawler.

"Now, Mr. Anderson helped everyone shoot. He was holding the bow string, right?"

"He was. He helped all of the girls."

During the cross-examination, Lawler noticed Wright's mother making hand signals to her daughter telling her what responses to give. After asking the judge to stop the communication, Lawler continued.

"Mr. Anderson used his other hand to steady Ms. Garner's, is that right?"

Wright said it was.

"Then which hand did you see grab Ms. Garner?"

"It was probably the hand on the string after she shot."

"You were standing on the side of Ms. Garner. Her back was to you and Mr. Anderson's back was to you. He had to put his arm over Ms. Garner's shoulder to steady her. His body would have blocked your view. How did you see him grab her breast?"

"I didn't. Terri told me he had later."

The prosecution rested its case with their alleged victims discredited. The case was almost over, but Lawler wanted a full vindication for Anderson. To do that, he needed to prove the girls' conspiracy.

He began by calling Counselor Allen to the stand. Allen explained, in detail, how the girls came to her office for four consecutive weeks. It was only during the fourth visit that they made their allegations of sexual abuse.

Lawler asked Allen if she was sure of the date that the girls made the allegation and she said she was. Lawler then read a portion of the girls' testimony to Allen, regarding the first alleged sexual assault.

"If your records are correct, the girls were assaulted before their third visit to your office. Did they mention anything about it to you?"

"No," Allen answered. "They didn't say anything until a week later."

"During the third meeting you told them they needed to have a very good excuse to get out of gym. If they were being sexually assaulted, why do you think the girls didn't tell you then?"

"Because I believe the girls are making up these allegations. I didn't believe them when they first brought them to my attention and I don't believe them now."

Lawler called Pike's Peak's health teacher, Gary Mullen, to the stand. Lawler's investigator had uncovered a possible link in the girls' conspiracy.

"You have Ms. Garner, Ruff and Wright in your class, is that correct?"

"Yes. I also have several of the witnesses in this case in my class."

"One week before the alleged victims made their allegations, did you show a film in your class?"

"I did. It was on who to talk to if you are molested."

"And Ms. Garner, Ruff and Wright watched the filmstrip. Did they say anything to you after watching it?"

"No. They left for drama class."

The Verdict and the Aftermath

The defense rested, and the case moved to closing arguments. Lawler explained how the girls had made up their stories to get back at Anderson for making them run laps.

"They all told the same story because they wrote their statements at the same time," Lawler said. "Principal Danser put a bunch of girls in a room, alone, and expected them not to talk. Then they all come out with the same statement. Should anyone be surprised?"

Lawler continued to hammer away at the prosecution's case.

"Short of Mr. Anderson being born with a genetic mutation, a third hand, could my client grab the breasts of any female on the archery range? You saw the alleged victims try to pull back the bow. They couldn't do it without help. How in the world was he holding the bow, pulling the string and grabbing their breasts at the same time? The answer is as simple as the lie you all are being fed by the prosecution. He couldn't have, and he didn't," Lawler reasoned.

Lawler reminded the jurors that each girl had recanted most of their stories on the witness stand. He asked the jury, "If the girls were lying about part of their stories, how could the rest of their testimony to be believed?"

Lawler finished his closing arguments with a plea to the jury to set an innocent man free. Three hours later, the jury did as he asked. Anderson was acquitted on all counts.

"The case was far from over," Lawler said. "Danser and the district were not about to let it go."

The school district kept Anderson on suspension for another year. During that time, Anderson's teacher certification came close to expiring.

"Principal Danser tried to use the certification issue as a back door to firing Anderson," Lawler explained. "An expired teaching license is grounds for termination. The principal of the school in which you are employed has to sign off on the renewal. Danser was refusing to sign it. I sent him a letter threatening legal action, and he resolved the matter."

Anderson was re-instated by the district but assigned to a different school.

Anderson's woes followed him to the new school. A week after he started, a student complained that Anderson had tied her shoes too tightly. On a recommendation by the school district's counsel, Anderson was suspended again.

"The CEA had witnessed too many violations of Anderson's rights by then," Lawler said. "We were working on filing a civil suit against the school district, but the lawsuit was never filed. The district pre-empted the suit with an agreement. Anderson was given a job at the administration building for three years – until his retirement. Because of the mental stress the case caused him, he was probably headed for a disability retirement anyway. He couldn't have taken much more."

For Anderson, his acquittal of criminal charges and the settlement of his potential civil suit were hollow victories. He would never teach again.

"We won an acquittal, but this case still bothers me," Lawler said. "The students that admitted making up this stuff about Anderson were never punished. The only thing this case did was illustrate that students can manufacture false allegations against a teacher and get away with it. If the law was changed to make students liable for false allegations, I think some of these cases would never get started."

Guilty Until Proven Innocent

Chapter 2
Lisa Ridgeway

The Beginning

Lisa Ridgeway can't say she wasn't warned. The town's slogan, *500 Happy People and a Few Sore Heads*, is written in bold, black letters on the Harrisburg town sign. Most people chuckle at the motto as they drive past the sign on Interstate 76. In 1991, for Ridgeway, the motto would prove to be no laughing matter.

Middle-aged and slightly overweight, Ridgeway was a single woman who worked as a high school special education teacher. She devoted all of her energy to her students.

Ridgeway hugged students who, she thought, needed positive reinforcement. She also regularly attended athletic events and extra curricular activities in which her students were involved. Even at Ridgeway's home, her students were never forgotten. The door to her tiny apartment was always open to a student in crisis.

Often, students would stop by Ridgeway's home, and she would drink coffee with the teens while they told her about their school problems or relationship woes. Her workdays were long and exhausting, but Ridgeway always had a sense of personal fulfillment. Ridgeway counted herself among the happy people of Harrisburg and couldn't fathom why the town sign warned of a few sore heads.

In late November 1991, she got her answer.

The morning that changed her life started like any other. She was making coffee and getting ready for school when her phone rang.

Sandra Lucci, her school's principal, was on the line and she sounded upset. Lucci was cryptic in her conversation with Ridgeway. She only told Ridgeway to meet with the Superintendent of Harrisburg schools, Douglas Padilla, immediately. When Ridgeway pressed for more information, Lucci said she couldn't discuss the situation and hung up.

At the time of the phone call, Ridgeway had been employed in the Warner County District for almost thirteen years. Harrisburg is a small community, so they shared teachers like Ridgeway with other small communities, but Padilla was still her boss. Ridgeway thought the request was unusual. She'd never been called to the Superintendent's office before, but she wasn't concerned about it.

Padilla, a short, skeletal man with thinning black hair, was seated behind his desk when Ridgeway arrived at his office. He motioned her to come inside and asked her to close the door behind her. Ridgeway knew there was a real problem.

Padilla skipped pleasantries and immediately told Ridgeway she was going to be placed under suspension due to pending allegations of sexual abuse against her. Ridgeway was stunned. She thought of all her interactions with students, trying to think of anything that might have been inappropriate, but couldn't think of anything.

Padilla refused to look her in the eyes as he spoke. Instead, his eyes seemed to bore a hole through the floor. When Ridgeway pressed for details, he told her to wait for the Warner County Sheriff's Office to call. He said he believed everything would be cleared up quickly.

The wait was excruciating for Ridgeway. She rarely left her home and when she did, she imagined strangers were staring at her, despite the fact the allegations hadn't been made public. In her mind, she had been branded a child molester. When Melinda Hanson of the Warner County Sheriff's substation finally called seven days later, Ridgeway hoped her ordeal was near an end. She drove directly to the substation to meet with the investigating officers.

At the substation, Hanson informed Ridgeway that three of her special education students, Kenny Safeway, Jason Olson and William Tiger, had alleged that she had inappropriately touched them in the classroom.

Compounding the situation, school counselor John O'Reilly claimed to have witnessed other incidents of inappropriate touching by Ridgeway in the past.

Questions of Employment Status

Ridgeway realized the full implication and seriousness of the charges against her and sought legal help. She called the CEA and was referred to Greg Lawler.

"I called the Sheriff's substation to get some facts in the case," Lawler said. "After we talked things through, they explained there wasn't a case against Ms. Ridgeway. They were sending it back to the school for them to deal with, which is standard practice since the school can still move to terminate even if the authorities don't file charges."

Lawler assumed the matter was resolved, but he was wrong. The school district opened their own investigation and in December 1991, they requested Ridgeway's resignation as a result of their investigation.

"A district will often take disciplinary action even if the police determine a crime hasn't been committed. The school district's evidentiary threshold is much lower than a criminal court's. Often, all it takes is a unsubstantiated allegation," Lawler explained. "The school district needs to prepare for the inevitability of a law suit filed by the parents of the allegedly abused students. If a school board does not take action by requesting a termination hearing, that fact will come out in court. If a teacher isn't disciplined, it looks like the district doesn't care, which possibly raises the dollar amount of any punitive damages awarded by the jury in the civil suit."

When Ridgeway's resignation was requested, Lawler was informed that the school board would attempt to terminate Ridgeway without a formal due process hearing. If the school board terminated Ridgeway without a hearing, Lawler would have to file with the district court requesting a court order demanding the school district grant her a hearing pursuant to her rights. Getting the courts to intervene in school business is tough. Courts are hesitant to interfere in the day-to-day operations of school districts, particularly in a small town.

"It takes a lot of courage on the part of the judge to grant such a request," Lawler said. "The court's findings are not based on the entire evidence of the case, but on teacher status. At this point, the defense hasn't even seen the school district's investigation, so the motion has to be argued solely because the due process rights of the accused have been violated."

In situations like Ridgeway's, the school district is not required to turn over the findings of its investigation to defense counsel if the school district has not submitted those records to the District Attorney.

"Some school districts will share the investigation records," Lawler said. "However, that only happens when there's solid evidence against the teacher. If there is evidence that refutes the allegations, school districts often will not share their findings with defense counsel. The school district had made up their mind and didn't want to give me any information that might be useful in future legal proceedings. This leaves teachers groping for answers that they don't know the question to. Without the facts, teachers cannot properly defend themselves."

Lawler attempted numerous times to examine the case against his client, but was denied access by the district. He needed to find a legal back door to look at the evidence the district had against Ridgeway. In the meantime, Lawler hired his own investigator to turn-up evidence supporting Ridgeway.

"To get access to the records, I needed to obtain a hearing and have the school district make them part of the hearing record," Lawler explained. "There was a strong probability the district's attorney wouldn't enter the files into evidence, so I hoped a witness would allude to the school district's investigation. Either way, I'd have to wait until the hearing to be granted access."

While Lawler prepared for the coming legal battle, Ridgeway's students and friends took the matter into their own hands. More than a hundred letters were written to the school district, asking for Ridgeway's reinstatement. Even the students who made the initial allegations began talking to other students about their desire to see Ridgeway in the classroom again. Some students attempted to talk to Principal Lucci, but she turned them away.

Despite her embarrassment, Ridgeway refused to keep a low profile. She made repeated requests to the school district for any information, in addition to the three allegations, that supported the school district's upholding her suspension. She never received an answer.

Because the school district closed the lines of communication, Lawler's hand was forced. He filed a mandamus action, requesting that the district either put her back to work or give her a hearing pursuant to the Colorado Dismissal Law.

"Cases in which teachers have to get a court order for a hearing are rare," Lawler said. "Most school districts will move forward because they have the upper hand. Even if the teacher is successful at the termination hearing, the school board can still terminate the teacher's contract."

The hearing was set for May, 1992, but due to the complexity of the case, it was postponed until June, 1992.

Lawler states the school district didn't respond well to being pushed.

"Soon after the mandamus hearing date was set, Ridgeway received a letter from the school district saying that her contract was not being renewed. During the hearing it was revealed that, based on advice from the school district's attorney, they could wait until her contract expired and simply not renew it. This would prevent the school district from having to give her due process. That made it clear to me that the school district was not dealing with her in good faith."

The Harrisburg School District's attorneys used the contract expiration to circumvent a dismissal hearing. They argued that since Ridgeway was a shared employee and not an employee of the Harrisburg School District, she was a probationary teacher and not entitled to a hearing.

Lawler successfully challenged the finding in the Warner County Courts. On July 29, 1992, Warner County District Court Judge Addams ordered, "Miss Ridgeway was a teacher of thirteen years, and she should not be terminated unless she was given an opportunity for a hearing."

Media Coverage and the Public

Two days later, Lawler was not surprised to learn the school district was asking the judge to reconsider his ruling. The district's reasoning angered Lawler. The school district was now arguing Ridgeway was a clear and present danger to the children in the school.

The judge refused to reconsider his ruling, but the damage was done. *The Greeley Tribune* and several local papers had picked up the story and quoted the school district's court filing as reading that Ridgeway was a threat to her students. The news articles all failed to mention the Warner County sheriff's office found all charges to be without merit.

"School districts know that teachers are vulnerable to adverse publicity," Lawler said. "The school district's motion was an attempt to use the media to intimidate my client."

Ridgeway's friends and family members read the stories that described her inaccurately as a child abuser.

The stories portrayed her to be an unstable pedophile. Thinking about the impact the stories had on her family, the stories made it tough for her to remain balanced.

During this dark period, Ridgeway received a glimmer of hope from the school district. In August, 1992, Ridgeway received a certified letter from Superintendent Padilla directing her, as an employee of the school district, to report for duty. Ridgeway thought her nightmare was over.

"The day I received the letter, I rushed to the store and bought school supplies, notebooks, pens and the like and began preparing lesson plans," Ridgeway said. "I was excited to return to the classroom."

She couldn't wait to see her students' smiling faces, but they were smiles she would never see again.

On August 21, 1992, Ridgeway received a second certified letter from Superintendent Padilla placing her on administrative leave, with pay, until further notice.

"The district was playing with her emotions," Lawler said. "They were trying to make her surrender. It was emotional warfare."

Outraged, Ridgeway decided it was time to speak out publicly.

On the front page of the Sunday edition of the *Denver Post*, Ridgeway gave her first public statement about her situation.

The story chronicled the plight of teachers falsely accused of inappropriate touching and their battles to regain their professional careers. Although the story mentioned other current Colorado cases of teacher abuse, Ridgeway's story was featured prominently. The news article explained, in-depth, how Ridgeway's right to a fair hearing had been denied her.

A swell of support formed for Ridgeway, thanks in part to the article. On September 8, approximately 150 parents and students packed the Harrisburg school board room, demanding Ridgeway be returned to the classroom. The meeting was filled with emotion. Students were angry and bitter about the time Ridgeway had been absent from class. They all believed she had been withheld from them unfairly.

Although no one stood up and spoke against Ridgeway, the overwhelming community support failed to move the school board. Many on the board sat with crossed-arms, blatantly unwilling to listen to the community. A petition with nearly three hundred parent signatures was submitted to the Board of Education for Ridgeway's re-instatement. The meeting was brought to a close.

The next day, an article appeared in the *Greeley Tribune* condemning the actions of the school board as a witch-hunt. That same day, the school board held its monthly meeting. Again, students and parents filled the room in support of Ridgeway, but the school board attorney precluded any statements from the floor at that meeting.

Ridgeway found the community support emotionally uplifting, but she also discovered how fickle the media's coverage of her situation could be. On September 11, 1992, the *Greeley Tribune* published an article quoting the school district's motion for reconsideration of the ruling. The article purported that having Ridgeway in a classroom was dangerous. The same paper that had once labeled her treatment by the district as a witch-hunt had smeared her name yet again.

"It appeared that the newspapers put their finger in the wind to determine the way public sentiment is blowing," Lawler said. "By covering stories the way the public wants them to, newspapers generate a greater readership, and by direct correlation, ad sales. That was the reason behind the shifting media coverage."

Through all the turmoil, Ridgeway had been unable to tell the school board her side of the story. On September 15, 1992, nearly ten months after the allegations against Ridgeway surfaced, the school board granted her a chance to defend herself.

"This was a teacher who gave thirteen years of her life to the school district and that was the first time an administrator talked to her about the situation," Lawler said. "The fact is, everything was so far along, and nothing productive could have come from the meeting. They were already in a lynch-mob mode. The only things they were missing were the torches and the pitchforks." Despite his frustration, Lawler used the meeting to his advantage.

He spoke to Superintendent Padilla and the school district's attorneys. Lawler emphasized he was willing to take the case as far as necessary to return Ridgeway to her students.

Lawler's statements had an impact with the school district. When the teacher dismissal hearing finally began on April 19, 1993, the district's attorneys admitted they began their investigation on September 15, 1992, after their meeting with Lawler.

"The meeting with the district was simply to gather dirt on Ridgeway," Lawler said. "I hoped it was to try and put her back in the classroom. Everything was blown way out of proportion. I think the school district knew then that the charges were false, but they had to cover themselves from a possible civil action by Ridgeway."

The Trial

On December 22, 1992, Ridgeway was contacted and told the school board was bringing dismissal charges. The hearing date was set for April 19, 1993. Lawler's investigation had turned up the evidence that was needed to clear his client's name. He was looking forward to the hearing.

The hearing opened with James Mathau and Malcolm Redd representing the school district and Lawler representing Ridgeway. Hearing Officer Lisa Winsome presided over the hearing.

"We went through several procedural motions during the first day," Lawler said. "We didn't start hearing from witnesses until the afternoon session."

Mathau opened the proceedings by calling Superintendent Padilla as his first witness. Padilla explained how three students went to counselor John O'Reilly to complain they weren't being taught in class. The students also alleged that other students, not enrolled in their class, were entering the classroom to talk to Ridgeway, which was taking away from their class time.

"Ridgeway was the Spirit Club sponsor," Lawler explained. "The students that entered her class were there on school business, and O'Reilly was aware of that. It came out during cross-examination that he had failed to mention that fact when he notified the principal of the allegations."

Mathau asked Padilla how that meeting turned into an allegation of abuse. Padilla claimed O'Reilly pressed the students for more details about the classroom situation, and one of the boys stated Ridgeway made him uncomfortable.

O'Reilly's report stated the boy claimed Ridgeway would touch him on the inside of his thigh. The report was given to Principal Lucci, and she called Padilla. Padilla stated he had no choice but to open an investigation and suspend the teacher.

Mathau called Counselor O'Reilly to the stand and he corroborated Padilla's testimony about the report. O'Reilly elaborated by claiming that he had seen Ridgeway hug several students after a football game. O'Reilly alleged Ridgeway pressed her bosom into the student's chest and held it there for several seconds. O'Reilly testified that he had seen similar incidents of the same action at school.

"We never disputed Ridgeway hugged her students," Lawler said. "She was working with kids that needed extra attention. Some of her students functioned at a higher level than others did, but Ridgeway thought that all of her students needed emotional support to boost their self-esteem. I needed to show, on the record, that her hugs were not sexual in nature."

Over the next five days of the hearing, Mathau called students who testified about hugs given to them by Ridgeway. The three accusing students then testified Ridgeway's classroom door would be shut during the day, and she would hug or touch them behind the closed door.

On April 27, 1993, Lawler got a chance to present Ridgeway's side of the case. He began by calling school counselor O'Reilly. Lawler had cross-examined O'Reilly after his direct examination, but Lawler's investigator had uncovered new information about the counselor.

During testimony, O'Reilly admitted he didn't like Ridgeway. O'Reilly attributed the dislike to the closed classroom door and the hugging.

Lawler asked O'Reilly to demonstrate the hugs he witnessed and O'Reilly complied. During the demonstration, Lawler asserted the hugs were platonic in nature. Because of Ridgeway's size, Lawler demonstrated it was impossible for Ridgeway's bosom not to touch the students' chests while hugging them from the front.

"He spent five minutes trying to demonstrate that it was possible not to touch a student's chest," Lawler said. "When he couldn't demonstrate that, he fell back on his argument that a teacher should never touch a student."

Lawler wondered why O'Reilly viewed the hugs as sexual and asked O'Reilly if he thought hugging a student, at any time, was inappropriate. O'Reilly replied it was. O'Reilly testified that Principal Lucci and he had warned Ridgeway about touching students on numerous occasions.

"So any teacher that hugs a student is engaged in inappropriate conduct. Would taking a student to a strip club qualify as inappropriate?"

"It would," O'Reilly answered.

Lawler introduced evidence showing O'Reilly had taken several male students to a local strip club.

"Several student witnesses had given me sworn statements that O'Reilly had taken a group of students to a local strip club," Lawler said. "O'Reilly gave the boys dollar bills and helped the teens place the dollars in the g-string of a stripper dancing in the middle of the group. The boys also informed me that the counselor bought beer for the group that evening."

O'Reilly left the stand discredited. He later resigned his position, but was rehired within the district at a different school.

Lawler questioned Padilla.

"What evidence do you have showing Ms. Ridgeway inappropriately touched the students, besides the testimony of Mr. O'Reilly?" Lawler asked the Superintendent.

"I have all the evidence I need in my investigation files," Padilla said, pointing to the black binders containing the investigation records Lawler had been denied access.

Lawler immediately made a motion to have access to the records. Since Padilla alluded to them during testimony, they were fair game. Hearing Officer Winsome agreed and Lawler finally had the access he'd been seeking for two years.

The hearing was recessed to provide Lawler a chance to look at the investigation records. The records contained numerous statements, from both faculty and students, exonerating Ridgeway.

When the hearing resumed, Lawler had the exculpatory statements added to the record. He questioned Padilla again.

"You don't like Ms. Ridgeway," Lawler said. "Why is that?"

"Because women shouldn't wear pant suits – especially when they are overweight," Padilla answered. "It's unprofessional."

The hearing was adjourned for the day. The next day, Lawler received confirmation the Padilla testimony had struck a chord with Hearing Officer Winsome.

"She showed up in court the next day wearing a pant suit. It may have been a coincidence, but I think it sent a message to Padilla," Lawler said.

Lawler spent the next two days calling student witnesses he had discovered through the district's investigation record. Every witness testified to Ridgeway's innocence.

Most witnesses refuted the claims of inappropriate touching. Two of Ridgeway's students claimed the alleging boys were angry with Ridgeway for disciplining them. Safeway, the boy who alleged Ridgeway touched the inside of his thigh, had been sent out of the classroom for disruptive behavior the day before making the accusations to O'Reilly.

Lawler uncovered even more damaging evidence of a conspiracy by the school district to unjustly terminate Ridgeway.

Safeway had been placed into an internship in the principal's office during the months leading up to the trial. Previously, the internship had gone to honor students. During his time in the principal's office, the school district's attorney made a daily two-hour trip from Denver to the school and coached Safeway on what to say during trial. An office secretary corroborated Safeway's testimony.

Immediately after the dismissal hearing, Safeway lost his internship and the job was given to the eventual class valedictorian.

Lawler concluded his case, believing Ridgeway's name was cleared. Two weeks later, his belief was confirmed.

The Ruling

Hearing Officer Winsome entered a finding of fact completely vindicating Ridgeway. To order the teacher's reinstatement, she first had to find that Ridgeway was a non-probationary teacher of the Warner County School District.

Winsome ruled that O'Reilly had not taken proper notes during his initial interviews and most of his testimony was based on personal feelings. O'Reilly also did not fully describe the allegations to Principal Lucci when he first reported the incident which violated Colorado law. Personal bias and the fact that Ridgeway had not been given a fair chance to respond to the accusations seriously contaminated the investigation.

Her last finding, regarding the recommendation by district counsel to let Ridgeway's contract expire, was that the school district's actions had been solely designed to avoid giving Ridgeway her due process. Winsome stated that the manner in which the district conducted the investigation was detrimental to the teacher, students and the process.

In her ruling, Winsome wrote that, "All charges the district made were unfounded or fabricated." Hearing Officer Winsome recommended the immediate retention of Ridgeway.

Despite the finding, Ridgeway never set foot in a Warner County classroom again. Her experience embittered her and left her feeling unwanted. She could not return to the classroom and be effective. Lawler and Ridgeway sued the school district. The civil suit was settled for an undisclosed amount of money.

Ridgeway continues to work in education as a private tutor.

"The Ridgeway case is an example of a system that provided a teacher with little means of defending herself," Lawler said. "By denying me access to the investigation, the district was able to hide evidence of her innocence, evidence the district had all along. If the legal technicality that allowed the school district to keep their investigative records to themselves were changed, Ridgeway would still be teaching today."

Chapter 3
Joanna Chapel

The Beginning

Joanna Chapel's stomach curled in fear as the two boys circled each other menacingly. Chapel warned the two high school sophomores to stop and return to class, hoping to end the incident before blows were traded. The boys ignored her order and began pushing each other hard in the chest.

At 98-pounds, Chapel was no match for the young men. Johnnie Sykley and Russ Meyers were varsity football players at Quincy High School in Washington County, Colorado. Each boy weighed nearly 200-pounds, mostly muscle. Chapel had seen the boys yelling at each other earlier. Now, following their lunch period, she saw the boys' notebooks on the floor, ready to square off. They were directly in front of Mike Russell's classroom.

"I recognized one of the boys as one I had accompanied to the office on a prior occasion when a substitute teacher had asked me to take him to the office because he had been totally out of control," Chapel said. "Also, I had often observed this particular class's rowdy and disruptive behavior in the hallways at the end of their lunch period because their teacher, Mr. Russell, never seemed to be able to return to his classroom before his students after the lunch period."

Chapel looked for Russell, but he was not in sight. Chapel yelled for help, hoping another teacher would step in to break up the fight. A large crowd of students had gathered to watch the two boys beat each other, and her pleas for help could not be heard over the catcalls and taunts coming from the crowd.

Chapel watched in horror as Meyers suddenly lashed out. He threw a hard uppercut into the chin of Sykley. Sykley reared back and retaliated with a strong blow to Meyers' gut. The crowd went wild, howling for blood. Chapel knew the boys could get seriously hurt if she allowed the fight to continue. She steeled her nerves and stepped between the two combatants.

Meyers threw a punch that whistled past her ear. She heard a sickening thud as the punch found its mark below Sykley's right eye. Sykley shoved Chapel hard to the ground and advanced on Meyers. He swung wildly and missed. Meyers countered with a hard left to Sykley's temple.

Chapel staggered to her feet and put her hands on Sykley's chest. She pushed with all her weight, trying to back up the angry young man. She felt like she was pushing against a brick wall. Chapel took her hands off the boy's chest, and then slammed them back on him again. Sykley stumbled backwards, a look of shock on his face.

"Sykley began to move towards me. I remember my strongest thought was that [Sykley] was either going to strike me or strike [Meyers] and continue to fight," Chapel wrote, in her written statement to Quincy High Assistant Principal John Garcia. "I made a split-second decision to shove [Sykley] away from me. At that point in time, the students who had been watching the fight and cheering the boys on, all began to yell that a teacher had hit a student."

Chapel listened to the accusing chants of abuse, stunned. She watched, frozen, as Dave Jesper, the shop teacher, encircled his mammoth arms around Sykley. He had heard the commotion on his way back from lunch and came to help. Jesper lifted the boy off his feet and began dragging him to the office. Mike Carter, Jesper's friend and fellow shop teacher, restrained Meyers.

Chapel thanked Carter and Jesper as they were leaving, then took a deep breath.

"It was then that Mr. Russell appeared from lunch and I told him that I had just intervened in a fight with two of his emotionally and behaviorally disturbed students," Chapel wrote. "After informing Mr. Russell of the situation, I next found Assistant Principal John Garcia and apprised him of the situation."

The Complaint

After leaving Garcia's office, Chapel went to find the two shop teachers, who were on their planning break. She found them in the faculty lounge, discussing the fight. The two men asked Chapel what had transpired. Chapel told them the entire story. Jesper told Chapel he didn't know a fight was under way until he heard the students screaming about a teacher hitting someone. He offered to make a statement to Garcia backing up her story. Chapel thanked him but told him that wouldn't be necessary.

Before Chapel left for the day, Garcia paid a visit to her classroom. Garcia informed Chapel that he needed a written statement from her about the incident. Sykley had received a black eye in the fight and was claiming Chapel had given him the bruise. Garcia told Chapel that Sykley was claiming she had used excessive force to break up the fight and had punched him in the eye with a closed fist.

"Garcia told me that he planned to call Sykley's parents and would talk with them," Chapel said.

Garcia told Chapel that allegations of abuse have to be reported to the police but, because the complaint was about how she broke up the fight, the school would deal with the matter internally.

Chapel gave the school her statement and thought the matter was resolved. The day after the fight, November 14, 1989, Chapel realized her ordeal was just beginning.

The District's Investigation

Because of the fight, both boys were suspended. Johnnie Sykley's father picked him up from school and drove him home. The ride home was filled with a tense silence. Finally, Johnnie's father broke the silence by teasing Johnnie about his black eye.

Johnnie didn't laugh. Instead, he told his father he hadn't been fighting. Johnnie claimed he had been play fighting, and Chapel had misunderstood what was going on. He told his father that Chapel had thrown him into a locker and punched him in the face.

Johnnie's father was stunned by his son's statement. The next day, he called Assistant Principal Garcia to make an abuse report.

Garcia arranged for a meeting between Chapel and the Sykleys.

"Mr. Garcia told me that the Sykleys were concerned that I had punched their child in the face. Mr. Garcia wanted me to tell them what had happened," Chapel said.

At the meeting, Chapel explained her actions to the parents of Johnnie Sykley. The boy's mother and father listened without asking any questions. When Chapel was finished with her explanation, the parents shook hands with her and left. They never told Garcia or Chapel that they had already filed a child abuse complaint with the Washington County Sheriff's Office.

"Wednesday, November 15, at the end of the school day, Mr. Garcia approached me in the hallway and handed me Detective Sharon French's business card. He told me Sykley's parents had filed a complaint and that he was sorry. He said he'd done all he could, but Sykley's parents had called her on Monday – the day of the fight," Chapel said.

Garcia told Chapel to call French and schedule an interview. Chapel called the detective the next day. French wanted Chapel to come down to the police station to talk about the incident, but Chapel refused. Chapel reasoned she could give the same information over the phone.

"I was extremely irate by this point," Chapel said. "I still had to deal with a situation which I felt had been resolved."

French relented and took Chapel's statement over the phone. After Chapel finished giving her version of the events, French informed her that the complaint would have to be forwarded to the District Attorney's Office and they would make the decision on whether or not to file charges. French expected a decision to be made by Monday.

Prior to interviewing Chapel, French had already talked to witnesses of the fight. All of the students she interviewed denied a fight had taken place. French highlighted a statement in her report to the District Attorney by Tracy Smith, a girl in Sykley's SIEBD class.

"Sykley and Meyers were fake fighting…you know…playing. Ms. Chapel came over and told them to stop. When they didn't, she threw Sykley against a locker. He said something to her and she punched him."

French had also interviewed Sykley and Meyers. Both boys claimed they hadn't been fighting. Meyers told French he'd seen Chapel throw Sykley against a locker but hadn't seen her punch him because her back was to him.

"At this point, I became really concerned," Chapel said. "I wasn't worried about legal bills since I was a member of the CEA, but I was worried about the damage to my career. I knew criminal charges could lead to the loss of my teaching license. I called the CEA, and Greg Lawler took my case. He walked me through what would happen and explained the ramifications of a police report, something no administrator had done for me. I was floored by what could happen. My name was going to be placed in the abuse registry of Colorado, and the allegations would show up during future background checks. I told Greg I not only wanted to be cleared of wrongdoing, but I wanted my record expunged."

On November 15, the Washington County Sheriff's department filed formal charges against Chapel. Because she was charged with misdemeanor assault, she wasn't arrested.

"This was a teacher that broke up a fight between two boys that were twice her size," Lawler said. "I didn't think charges should have been filed because she was going about the normal course of her duties. The sheriff's office was getting pressure from the parents to charge her, and they had corroborating witnesses. If one of the boys had been seriously injured, my client and the school would have been held liable in a civil suit. She did the only thing she could. I took the case not only to protect my client, but also to protect other teachers who may find themselves falsely accused. I was also worried because I could see the chilling effect that the charges were having on other teachers at Chapel's school."

Lawler explained that the other combatant, Russ Meyers, was involved in a fight the day after charges against Chapel were filed. According to Lawler, teachers were present during the fight and refused to break it up.

"Not only did the incident show that Sykley and Meyers were really fighting, it demonstrated the fear Chapel's charges placed upon every teacher. They were paralyzed. The teachers couldn't do their job for fear of criminal charges."

The students exacerbated the situation. When they heard about the charges against Chapel and that she hadn't been suspended, they threatened to walk out of class.

"The students were angry," Lawler said. "They reasoned that if they hit anyone, they would be suspended with no questions asked. The kids at Chapel's school saw her treatment as a double standard. They didn't know the facts of the case. They just saw a teacher still on the job that allegedly had struck a student."

Charges and Chaos

Lawler immediately contracted the services of an investigator. He needed to find a corroborating witness for Chapel's version of the events and prove the boys were lying. Lawler was curious about witness statements that claimed the two boys were roughhousing, not fighting. After meeting Chapel in person, Lawler wondered how a teacher of Chapel's size had thrown a student, who was more than twice her size, into a locker.

"I think Sykley was embarrassed he lost the fight and blamed Chapel," Lawler said. "He needed to save face with his peers."

While Lawler prepared a defense, the school district began an investigation of its own. School district officials were concerned that Assistant Principal Garcia hadn't followed school policy and notified the police when the allegations first surfaced. Following the district's investigation, no action was taken against Garcia. The District Attorney's Office did take action, though. Garcia was charged with failing to report child abuse, a misdemeanor offense.

"This is one of the few incidents where a school supported a teacher," Lawler said. "The repercussions Garcia endured show why school districts suspend teachers, even if they are innocent. If administrators side with the teacher, they risk being drawn into the legal proceedings themselves."

While Lawler and his investigator sorted through the conflicting accounts of the fight, Chapel wasn't sitting idly by. She began asking her superiors tough questions about Sykley and Meyers.

"When I learned Russ Meyers had beaten up another student, Mr. Jesper told me Johnnie Sykley routinely picked fights. I asked Principal Miller, Garcia's boss, about the boys," Chapel said. "He acted like he'd never heard of them. After that conversation, I discovered that both boys had been very big troublemakers, and Dr. Miller definitely knew who they were. I had the support of Mr. Garcia, but I think Dr. Miller was trying to wash his hands of it."

Chapel was frustrated and asked why Russell was late coming back from lunch that day.

"Dr. Miller told me things like that happen," Chapel said. "I've been a teacher for fifteen years, and I can tell you that just doesn't happen. It was clear Principal Miller wasn't going to fix the problem. I knew that if I didn't change the system somehow, it was just a matter of time before another teacher faced abuse charges."

Lawler's Investigation

The case proceeded to trial rapidly. According to Lawler, the case consisted of Sykley's word against Chapel's.

"In physical abuse cases, there's very little evidence," Lawler said. "The only way to mount a defense is to bolster your client's credibility. To do that, I needed to show Sykley had a history of violence, and that Ms. Chapel's side of the story was the only logical explanation."

Lawler's investigator uncovered evidence of Sykley's past disruptive behavior.

"We discovered that a month prior to the fight, a group of students got rowdy on a school bus on the way home from a field trip," Lawler said. "One of the students was Johnnie Sykley. He was standing up, yelling at another student. A teacher, Joan Shaw, was on the bus and yelled at Sykley to sit down. Sykley resisted and started cussing at Shaw. The teacher pushed Sykley back down in his seat. Sykley yelled, 'Ouch!' When that happened, the rest of the students began chanting 'Sue Shaw! Sue Shaw!' Sykley then told the teacher he would tell everyone he had been punched and get Shaw fired. The students knew the legal ramifications of an abuse complaint and were using it as a weapon…a weapon they weren't afraid to use against my client."

Lawler also found a district policy prohibiting anyone from standing and watching a fight. An infraction led to an immediate suspension.

"If the students admitted they were watching a fight, instead of a 'play fight', they faced a three-day suspension. The students had no incentive to tell the truth," Lawler said.

Lawler turned his findings over to the prosecutor. Lawler asked that all charges against his client be dismissed. He argued that even if Sykley sustained a bruise as a result of Chapel's actions, she was only doing her job.

Eventually, the District Attorney's Office agreed with that assessment. On February 24, 1990, all charges were dropped against Chapel and every record of the incident in her personnel file was expunged. Charges against Assistant Principal Garcia were subsequently dropped.

Chapel's Crusade

Lawler's portion of the case was concluded, but the fight was far from over for Chapel.

"Joanna Chapel was a strong woman. She didn't want to see any more teachers prosecuted for doing their job, and she was determined to do something about it," Lawler said.

Chapel began by trying to get the district to create a legal fund to pay the legal bills of teachers wrongly accused. Chapel's defense costs were picked up by the CEA, but Garcia's had not been. Union membership is not offered to administrators. Because the assistant principal was not a union member, he had paid thousands of dollars out of his own pocket for attorney fees, investigator fees and court costs. Chapel was instrumental in changing the district policy to reimburse the legal bills for school employees wrongly accused of crimes.

"The CEA assisted her in changing the policy," Lawler said. "There were a lot of legalities to work out, such as whether the defense costs were paid as the expenses occurred or reimbursed at the end of the proceedings. But, besides a few technical points, everything was worked out in a few weeks."

Chapel still wasn't satisfied. Since Colorado law requires teachers to keep order in the classroom, teachers need protection for actions they take to protect students. Over the next three months, she pressured Colorado Legislators for protection for teachers using reasonable force in the course of their duties. She also called newspapers and television stations arguing that a change to the law, to protect teachers in the course of their daily duties, was required.

Colorado's legislators were reluctant to draft legislation at first. But, due to the overwhelming news coverage Chapel generated for her cause, they drafted a bill protecting teachers in the normal course of their duties. In 1990, the legislation took effect.

Guilty Until Proven Innocent

Chapter 4
Janet Young

The Beginning

Janet Young had seen the small town of Mission, Colorado, undergo numerous changes. As a child, the small house she lived in with her two parents had been situated on a dirt road on the outskirts of town. Now, at age fifty, Young still lived in the small home. The road in front of the house was paved, a major artery in the growing plains town.

Young left Mission during her college years as a slim, bright and vivacious brunette. She returned to her hometown to work in the local high school after receiving her degree in music education from the University of Northern Colorado. The job opening became available just prior to receiving her degree, and Young saw the opportunity to teach in her hometown as fate.

After returning to Mission, Young first lived in a small one-bedroom apartment. Her parents offered Young free rent in their home, but the youthful teacher chose to assert her independence. The starting salary for teachers at the time was just less than fifteen thousand dollars, barely enough to make ends meet.

To keep from starving, Young ate dinner at her family home several nights a week. Young was an only child and her parents' health gradually deteriorated over the years. Young's salary increased over the years, and she used her resources to look after her ailing mother and father. After her parents' deaths, Young inherited her family home and took fastidious care of her mother's pride and joy, the flower garden. When she wasn't teaching her students the musical scales, she was worried about the pH scale of her potting soil.

Young's life was simple and idyllic. For the first eighteen

years of her career, she lived quietly. In 1993, two years away from her retirement, Young's once slim figure was rounded and her hair was flecked with gray. Young knew she was aging but saw her gray hairs as a symbol of wisdom and virtue.

Her neighbors thought of her in much the same way. Young volunteered for the Rotary Club, school bake sales, church groups and any other cause that needed a hard working pair of hands. Young envisioned the day she would finally be able to retire in Mission and dedicate her self full-time to worthy causes.

Young believed in small town values and wanted to pass her beliefs on to her students. She was unmarried, with no children and wanted her life's legacy to be the productive lives her students led. To Young, the most important thing she could pass on to her students was a respect for authority.

Young was a demanding teacher. Her music classes performed regularly at community events such as fairs and school concerts. Young demanded perfection from her pupils and to reach that level, they needed to pay attention in class. She had a reputation in her school as a good teacher but one who believed in discipline. Young's disciplinary measures would eventually strike a sour chord with school officials and lead to a legal battle that would reach the Colorado Supreme Court.

Reprimands and Repercussions

During October 1993, Young was preparing her students for a school concert. She was trying to teach them a song to be sung in Latin, but the students were having trouble with the piece. During the middle of a rehearsal, Young stopped the group at the beginning of a stanza. The class was off-key and had poorly enunciated numerous words.

Young started by correcting the class's pronunciation. She tried to loosen their tongues by having the students repeat a tongue twister – Rubber Baby Buggy Bumpers. Young listened as the class repeated the phrase, faster every time. During this exercise, the music teacher noticed one of her students, in the back row of the escalating choir stands, was not participating.

Jeremy Silva was normally a good student, but now his chin was tucked to his chest and his eyes were closed. Mid-term finals were approaching rapidly. Young assumed Silva had stayed up late studying for an exam. She wasn't angry with the sleeping student; he was normally a very respectful young man.

Young quietly walked behind the raised stands and gently grabbed Silva by the hair. She applied slight pressure to raise the student's head. The boy's eyes flickered open and he looked at her wearily. Young could see a look of embarrassment and shock wash over the young man's face. The boy stammered an apology, and Young told him everything was fine. She just needed him to pay attention. Silva nodded his head quickly in agreement and Young went on with her lesson.

Young didn't think about the incident until the next day. Principal Troy Brennan came to see her toward the end of the school day. Fearing Young would call his parents, something she often did when she disciplined a student, Silva went home and told his parents about the incident. Silva's mother, Melony Silva, was upset. Despite her son's explanation, Mrs. Silva thought that Young had pulled hard on her son's hair. Mrs. Silva reported the incident to the school.

Principal Brennan was bothered by the allegation but told Young he didn't believe the offense warranted a report to the authorities or a suspension. Instead, he was placing a letter of reprimand in her file. Because Young was close to retirement and she didn't anticipate further disciplinary problems, she did not object to the reprimand.

New Charges

Young continued teaching her students. A year went by, and she was getting ready to file her retirement papers. She would be eligible for her full retirement benefits at the end of the school year. Over the course of her final year, Young had scheduled three concerts. Because they would be her final performances, she wanted the concerts to be the most polished that they could be.

Young's classes performed for a nursing home in the middle of the first semester. The concert was one of the best performances she could remember. Of the two concerts remaining, Young's favorite was the Christmas performance. Most of Mission's small population would turn out for the event. The town's square would be decorated with garlands. Young could envision the twinkling red and green lights strung throughout the community's gathering place. In the center of the square would be a tall Christmas tree, decked with ornaments and candles securely attached to the branches.

The choir platform would be situated directly in front of the tree. Her choir would sing carols as the candles on the tree were lit. When the town's square was decorated for Christmas, it was a magical atmosphere for Young. She took special pride in the thought that her choir's songs would add to the enchantment of the evening. Unfortunately, Young would not be present for the concert.

One month before the Christmas concert, Young was helping her students perfect their performance. The class was singing beautifully, but she didn't want their grasp of the material to slip before the big night.

Young stood in front of the choir, directing the group. She'd cue the altos, sopranos and baritones to begin singing at the appropriate time with a wave of her pointer. The session was quickly ending, and Young could see that her student's attention span was waning. The lack of focus was particularly evident with the soprano section.

Twice already, the five girls that constituted the section had started singing before she cued them. Young asked the group to start the song over again. The class groaned but complied reluctantly. The song went smoothly until the soprano section again came in off cue. This time, Sallie Ray, the lead soprano, came in almost three beats too early. Young stopped the class and spoke to Ray.

"You need to concentrate," Young said, tapping Ray on the head with her pointer for emphasis. "We're almost through this. Just stay focused for a few more minutes."

Ray's face flushed crimson, and she refused to look Young in the eyes. A muscle just above Ray's left cheekbone trembled slightly. Young thought the girl was embarrassed and about to cry. She would later learn that Ray's reaction was one of pure anger.

When class was over, Ray wasted no time going to the office. The girl explained to Brennan that Young had rapped her with a pointer during class. The principal knew Young could be demanding, but wanted to get his teacher's side of the story before taking action. He immediately asked Young to come to the office.

Principal Brennan informed Young of the allegations and asked for her side of the story. Young confirmed Ray's assertion that she had tapped the girl on the head with her pointer. Young explained that she hadn't done it hard but had lightly tapped the girl to emphasize a point.

With a growing look of concern on his face, Brennan listened throughout the explanation. He told Young he would need to speak to district officials about the best way to handle the situation. Young was reminded she had a reprimand in her personnel file and that touching a student in the manner she had was inappropriate. Young was unapologetic but told Principal Brennan she understood he might have to take some from of disciplinary action. Brennan told Young he'd let her know what would happen by the end of the week.

Because Young was a teacher's union-member, Brennan suggested she contact the CEA for legal representation. Young thought she'd simply get a second reprimand in her file but contacted the CEA just in case. The CEA secretary gave her Lawler's number, and she called him.

"She told me she didn't think anything was seriously wrong," Lawler said. "Young fully expected the situation to resolve itself. Once she told me the history in her personnel file, I knew she was going to have big problems. With a letter of reprimand in her personnel file for a similar complaint, odds were that the district was going to suspend or terminate her. I explained that to Young, and I heard dead silence for what seemed like five minutes. When she finally said something, I could barely hear her. The reality of the situation had finally hit home."

Lawler knew termination was possible, but he still hoped for the best.

"She'd already acknowledged the complaint was valid," Lawler said. "If we had to go to trial or a termination hearing, I would be limited in the type of defense I could offer. Our best defense was to argue that while my client's conduct may have seemed inappropriate, it didn't warrant a termination."

Termination Hearing

No criminal charges were filed, but Lawler's prediction of termination came to fruition. The school board held an emergency meeting on December 2, 1993, and accepted charges to terminate Young's teaching contract. Lawler immediately requested a termination hearing and was granted it. Young was suspended with pay pending the outcome of the hearing.

"The process moved surprisingly fast at first," Lawler said. "The termination hearing was scheduled a month from the day of the dismissal charges."

During the termination hearing, evidence of the previous reprimand was presented to the hearing officer. The school district's attorney argued that the prior reprimand showed a pattern of behavior that required termination.

Both Ray and Silva testified at the hearing. Silva downplayed the previous offense and explained his hair hadn't been pulled. He testified that Young had simply woken him up during a class.

Ray was less forgiving in her testimony. The girl claimed Young had first yelled at her and then hit her on top of the head. Ray alleged the tap left a knot on her head.

"After Ray's testimony I called the school nurse to testify," Lawler said. "I asked if she'd treated Ray for a lump on the head. She answered by saying that she hadn't treated Ray in the entire time the girl had been in school. I then asked her parents if Ray had informed them about any injury. Both parents denied it. There was no record of an injury, and Ray hadn't reported a welt to Brennan. By introducing that testimony, I hoped to show Ray was embellishing her story."

The termination hearing concluded, but Lawler did not feel confident that the hearing officer would rule in his client's favor. He also worried that a ruling in his client's favor would be rejected by the school board and that his client would be dismissed.

"I immediately started to draft a filing for the Colorado Court of Appeals," Lawler said. "I knew there was a chance Young would be reinstated, but I wanted to be ready to move quickly."

While Young waited for the hearing officer's ruling, she tended to her flower garden and continued with her charitable activities. No one's business is private in a small town. Mission residents' conversations revolved around school events and Young's absence from the coming Christmas concert. Information that wasn't shared by the local newspaper was broadcast in whispers at the local coffee shop. Despite the gossip and controversy swirling around her, the community was supportive of Young.

"She hadn't been accused of molestation," Lawler explained. "That would have been a completely different situation. As it was, Mission residents thought my client had simply disciplined a student the way most of them wanted their own children disciplined. Mission is a small community, and the people there have small town values. They expected a certain level of discipline. My client had enormous community support, which I think helped her throughout the legal process."

Young had to wait more than three months for the hearing officer's ruling. During that time, she watched the Christmas concert from the cold of the town's square stands. Young's former students performed poorly, and she felt personally responsible for their sub-par display. Young was frustrated because she believed the group could have given the best concert the town had ever seen and was sad to see her students failing to live up to their potential, potential that could have been realized under her instructions.

"I think that experience motivated my client to keep fighting for her reinstatement, no matter what," Lawler said. "Young truly got a chance to see that her students needed her, and she had a small glimpse of what their lives were like without her. It was like a warped version of *It's A Wonderful Life*."

On March 2, 1994, Young was notified that the hearing officer had recommended her for reinstatement. She was elated by the news. She wanted a chance to finish an entire school year on a positive note. However, Young's plans were wasted.

"The hearing officer recommended reinstatement, but the school board still terminated her," Lawler said. "The school board is not obligated to follow the recommendation of the hearing officer. I had planned for this contingency. After we received notice of termination, We immediately filed an appeal with the Colorado Court of Appeals."

Colorado Court of Appeals

A case that reaches the appeals court takes years to reach a resolution. Lawler brought in Sharon Dreyer, a CEA appellate expert, to assist with the appeal. The two attorneys would not argue the motion for reinstatement for almost a year. During that time, Young filled her time by tending to her flowers and giving private music lessons. She had saved enough money over the years to live comfortably but wanted to see the legal process through to its conclusion.

"It was a matter of principle with her," Lawler said. "My client didn't think she'd done anything wrong and wanted to be told that by a court. She was an older woman, but she was full of spunk."

On December 22, 1994, Dreyer stood before the panel of judges and argued his client's case. A lawyer's time for argument is limited to fifteen minutes. During the time allotted, the judges are able to interrupt the attorney's time with questions about the case. Dreyer was interrupted numerous times.

"They asked a lot of questions about the reprimand," Lawler said. "They also questioned what actions constituted a terminable offense. The judges were worried about establishing a precedent that would enable teachers to abuse students and go unpunished. We could tell by the judges' questions that they were reluctant to rule in my client's favor."

Dreyer addressed the judges' concerns by explaining Young had only touched Ray's head lightly with the pointer. She stated that not reinstating Young would have a chilling effect on the relationship between students and teachers. Dreyer asserted teachers touch students in a playful and affectionate manner which helps to foster a feeling of community in both students and teachers.

Dreyer also argued that the type of interaction Young engaged in was common place in schools and that a ruling in the school district's favor would jeopardize the careers of hard working teachers across the state.

To address the judges' concerns about Young's reprimand, Dreyer pointed to Silva's testimony during the termination hearing, claiming the school district had overreacted to the incident.

The school district's position on the matter hadn't changed.

"They were consistent throughout the process," Lawler said. "I could have written their arguments for them. They believed a pattern of behavior by my client had been established and that they had sufficient grounds to terminate her contract. True to form, the school district's attorney argued the previous reprimand was enough, by itself, to terminate Young and that the school board had no choice but to terminate the teacher after her second offense. I thought we had countered those arguments successfully but was worried when the panel of judges interrupted the district's counsel only once. That told me that most of the judges had made up their mind before oral arguments, based on the court filings."

Lawler and Dreyer anticipated the ruling would go against his client but would have to wait until June 1, 1995, before the Colorado Court of Appeals published its decision.

"I was pleasantly surprised when the appeals court issued its ruling," Lawler said. "The court essentially agreed with our arguments that Young's actions did not warrant termination. They quoted the hearing officer's recommendation for reinstatement extensively. They stated that had the hearing officer made a grievous error, they would have had grounds to intervene. As it was, they found that the previous ruling had been a fair assessment of the situation."

The Colorado Supreme Court

The school district's attorneys disagreed with the decision of the Colorado Court of Appeals. The day of the lower court ruling, the school district filed an appeal with the Colorado Supreme Court. The district's request was granted, and the lower appeals court's ruling was stayed, pending the outcome of the new appeal.

During the time Lawler was drafting his response with Sharon Dreyer to the Colorado Supreme Court, the Joanna Chapel Legislation was enacted. Lawler hoped that the law change, instigated by his former client, would be enough to uphold the appeals court ruling. At a minimum, the new legislation gave him an additional argument for the appeals process.

On June 15, 1996, Dreyer presented her oral arguments to the Colorado Supreme Court. Because the court only rules based on State Constitutional or Legislative issues, Lawler and Dreyer continued their argument that Young had tapped Ray lightly and that the action didn't warrant termination and that the school district did not have sufficient legal grounds to get the ruling overturned.

"The school district was arguing, once again, that the prior reprimand gave them sufficient grounds for their actions. They claimed that if Young were reinstated, their ability to terminate teachers, for cause, would be jeopardized.

"To obtain a favorable ruling, we needed to meet two standards. First, we had to argue that despite the school district's legal arguments the case would have resulted in a similar ruling from the appeals court," Lawler said. "The basic argument was that the school district did not have sufficient grounds to overturn the lower court's ruling. Then we had to show that my client's actions were in the course of her duties and that she used reasonable force. Proving that Young's actions were responsible was the toughest obstacle to overcome. To uphold our client's re-instatement, the Supreme Court judges needed to find that Young's earlier actions, which resulted in a written reprimand, were responsible. That was a difficult argument to make."

The Colorado Supreme Court took a year to issue their finding. In early May, 1997, in a split decision, the court ruled in the district's favor. The court ruled that sufficient grounds for termination existed.

"If the case had simply been about my client tapping a student on the head, I think that the Chapel Legislation would have been very applicable," Lawler said. "Disciplining students clearly comes with the normal course of teaching duties. If it hadn't been for Young's disciplinary record, they may have ruled differently. The court held that the first offense rose to the level of a termination offense. To the court, anything that transpired after the first offense was moot."

The Final Resolution

Lawler regretted the impact the legal process had on Young's life but hoped teachers everywhere learned a lesson from her experiences.

"This case demonstrated to every teacher not to take any form of disciplinary action lightly," Lawler said. "Any blemish on a personnel record can be used against a teacher when they apply for a new job or have new complaints surface. The best course of action any teacher can take is to challenge unjust disciplinary actions before they become a part of their permanent record. I hope teachers everywhere take that lesson from this case."

Following the Supreme Court ruling, the school district asked to meet with Young and Lawler.

"I think the school district felt remorse for what happened to my client," Lawler said. "They fought us all the way to the Supreme Court to defend their right to terminate teachers for cause, in the future. It was never a personal vendetta against my client. They met with us to try to make the situation palatable for everyone and to appease the community that was still upset by her dismissal."

The school district's attorney informed Lawler and Young that since Young had only been a year away from retirement prior to her dismissal, she had garnered enough years of service to qualify for early retirement. The attorney explained that the school board had granted Young an early retirement, effective from the date of her termination.

"The case was never about money for my client, but the gesture went a long way to start the healing process for her," Lawler said. "By this time, Young had realized she could still be involved in her students' lives as a private tutor. When she wasn't tutoring, she planned to stay involved in local charities. By participating in the community, she hoped to show everyone in Mission that her head was still held high. She told me once that by dealing with the situation in a dignified manner, she would impart one last life lesson to her students."

Lawler followed up with Young to see how she was doing in the spring of 1998.

"She told me she was unhappy that her career ended the way it had, but that her flowers were blooming more brilliantly than they ever had before. She was making the best of a difficult situation."

Chapter 5
Aaron Marks

The Beginning

Mandee Fenster refused to work with Juan Mendoza again. The open insubordination was the last straw for Aaron Marks. As the head of the Special Education Department at Laughlin Elementary School in Aurora, Colorado, Marks taught students with mild to severe disabilities. He worked with them all and relied on paraprofessionals to help provide individual attention to his students.

Fenster, a heavy-set, middle-aged woman, with a poor attitude, thought she could choose the students with whom she worked. Fenster preferred to work with the mildly disabled students and had begun refusing to work with the severely disabled children. Fenster had confided in another paraprofessional, who had informed Marks that Fenster believed the severely handicapped students should never have been born or should have been aborted.

Marks had not acted on the information, choosing to give Fenster the benefit of the doubt. Now, after her third refusal to work with Juan in two weeks, Marks could not ignore her attitude problem. Marks asked another paraprofessional to cover his class and took Fenster to his small office, the size of a janitor's closet. Marks gestured for the paraprofessional to sit in a small chair and took a seat across the table from her.

Marks smoothed his ponytail, interlaced his fingers behind his thick black hair and leaned back in his chair.

"Are you happy here? Marks asked Fenster, trying to be pleasant.

Fenster took the opportunity to complain about Marks' frequent requests of her to work with the severely disabled students. Marks leaned back further in the chair as Fenster bent forward for emphasis, making her actions look more aggressive than she had intended. Fenster realized the message her body language was sending and relaxed in her chair, mirroring Marks' posture.

"We don't pick the students," Marks said. "The goal of the district is to mainstream disabled students, and our job is to work toward that goal. When I request that you work with a student, I'm doing so in my capacity as the head of the Special Education Department. It is not appropriate to question those directions. We both need to work together as part of a team and be on the same page."

Fenster disagreed vociferously.

"That's not what I was told during my hiring interview," Fenster argued, with anger seeping into her typically monotone voice. "I was hired by your predecessor, and he specifically told me that he would not have me work with the severely disabled. You've totally changed that and the routine he set – and his system worked. I'm not the only one upset by the change of the routine. By changing these kids' routines, you've thrown everything into chaos and made the job of us paraprofessionals tougher."

Marks sighed and for the first time in his two years at Laughlin, he wished he had taken his friend's offer to open their own flower arrangement business.

"I've been teaching for ten years," Marks said. "I might have only been at this school for two years, but I have more education and years of experience than you. My methods have been successful in the past, but to be successful, I need dedicated people supporting me. You have the potential to be a great paraprofessional, but I think that your attitude towards the students needs to improve.

"The changes I've made to the program are designed to allow every student to develop skills they'll need in life. My methods make these kids more self-sufficient and less reliant on others for assistance. That was not the goal of the previous program. The changes I've made have been approved by the district and follow guidelines established by the state. I know the changes have caused problems for you, but given time, the changes will make your job easier."

"That may be true," Fenster said. "But right now all I see is that your changes have caused problems for us paraprofessionals.

We've all talked about it and we all agree. We don't make enough money to compensate us for the troubles you've caused."

"I agree you're underpaid, even in the best of circumstances," Marks said. "But you knew the pay was minimal when you took the job. As a paraprofessional, you have to love what you do, and I don't sense that commitment from you. Maybe we should discuss ways to improve your feelings. Would you like to me to put together a training plan to assist you?"

"I don't see that I have a problem. I think the problem is with your changes."

"I take it from your response that you don't plan to change your attitude."

"I don't think my attitude is a problem," Fenster countered.

"Then I'm sorry," Marks said. "I'll be speaking with the principal this afternoon, and I have no choice but to request a reprimand be placed in your file."

"Do what you have to," Fenster said, her face flushing crimson. "I'll do what I think that I need to do."

Fenster walked from the room as Marks shook his head. Over the last two years, he'd worked to build a rapport with his staff. He ate lunch with the paraprofessionals daily and used the time to let the women vent or discuss issues in a non-threatening environment. Marks assumed that day's lunch would be tense.

That afternoon at lunch, Marks' paraprofessionals ate lunch before he arrived at the faculty lounge. When Marks went to sit down, the women each made an excuse to leave and left Marks to eat alone.

Prior to that, Marks had debated not requesting disciplinary actions against Fenster, but now he saw the potential for Fenster's attitude problem to permeate the rest of his staff. When the school day was over, Marks reluctantly went to Principal Peter White. Marks briefed White on his problems with Fenster and detailed Fenster's insubordination. He also informed White of Fenster's abortion comments to the other members of the staff. White agreed action needed to be taken. During the first period of the next day, White summoned Fenster to his office and formally reprimanded her.

Marks hoped that the disciplinary action would improve

Fenster's attitude, but it only seemed to make matters worse. Before, Fenster had been indifferent to students' needs. Now, she was sullen and inattentive. To help improve the paraprofessional's attitude, Marks tried to limit her contact with severely disabled students, but that was not always possible.

When Fenster was asked to work with students, such as Juan, she complied. However, Marks noticed her interaction with the boy was limited to making the student behave; she was not working with him on requested assignments.

The disciplinary action had also failed to keep Fenster's attitude from infecting the rest of his staff. Marks ate lunch alone on a regular basis, and his interactions with the paraprofessionals outside the classroom consisted of perfunctory greetings. Marks knew Fenster's resentment towards him was growing daily. In mid-October, Fenster found an outlet for her resentment.

The Complaint

In 2000, Laughlin Elementary School was overflowing with students. At the time, Colorado's strong economy was drawing families from surrounding states. Because of the growing student population and a lack of funds to remodel the school, Laughlin's administrators needed to be creative with the school's classroom space. Marks' classroom walls were not built of drywall. Instead, the walls consisted of fiberboard covered with a thin layer of padding.

The makeshift walls did not reach the ceiling. Instead, they were less than six-feet tall. The thin borders separated Marks' class from a class of fifth-grade students. Sound traveled easily between the rooms, and the faculty at the school had to make a concerted effort to keep noise down so other classes were not disturbed.

Marks' class was perpetually loud. Sounds of laughing, crying and talking flowed across the thin divider that separated the special education classroom from the rest of the school. Marks' colleagues tolerated the noise because they realized that the students in Marks' class could not always control themselves. The most disruptive student was Juan.

Juan's disabilities included Down's syndrome and a host of learning disabilities. Among the mentally challenged boy's greatest obstacles to learning were his language capabilities. Juan came from a family that spoke only Spanish in the home. Along with special education classes, the boy was enrolled as a student in the Aurora Public Schools English as a Second Language program. Because of his disability, Juan's English vocabulary was limited. Combined with the effects of his Down's syndrome, Juan's mental abilities were barely above those of the average kindergartner, despite the fact that he was twelve years old.

Juan knew he learned at a slower pace than his peers did, but he desperately wanted to be normal. In an effort to fit in with the other kids at school, Juan mimicked the actions and words of the students around him. Often, he repeated words and phrases he'd heard on the playground, without understanding their meaning.

Despite not fully understanding the images and actions depicted, Juan enjoyed watching television with his parents. The family's favorite show was *Law & Order*. Because of his television viewing, the boy had accused every student, paraprofessional and teacher in his class of crimes ranging from murdering the class goldfish to beating him up. With every accusation, Marks had to sit the boy down and explain that he was accusing people of things they hadn't done. Juan always apologized, and the comments were quickly forgotten.

On October 18, 2000, Juan's accusations were taken seriously. That day, Juan had been particularly difficult. After the first period of school, he had refused to follow his peers to their next class. Marks had asked Fenster to escort the boy to class. Once there, Juan was inattentive and disruptive. Marks had no choice but to discipline the boy by putting him in a "time out." The punishment meant that Juan had to sit in a chair, placed in the corner of the classroom, where he was unable to talk to the other students in the class.

Juan quickly grew bored and looked around the room for something to do. The boy looked across the partition and saw hands in the air. Thinking that he should do the same, Juan raised both of his arms straight up. The other students in Juan's class saw him raise his arms and tittered. Marks looked up from an exercise he was working on with several students and asked Juan what he needed. The boy didn't respond. Marks looked across the partition and immediately knew why the boy was raising his arms.

"You only raise your hand if you need something or want to say something," Marks told the boy. Marks' comments went unacknowledged by Juan. The boy kept his arms raised. Marks tried again to explain the reason for a raised hand to the boy, this time in Spanish. Juan still did not respond. Marks laughed and walked over to Juan.

Marks took Juan's hands in his, lowered them to chest level and clapped them together. He then placed Juan's hands in the boy's lap. To Marks' surprise, Juan's eyes filled with tears. He started to cry hard and loud.

Hearing the clap and then crying, Fenster came running into the classroom. Fenster told Marks she was going to take Juan to the bathroom to calm him down. Marks thought Fenster's actions were surprisingly empathetic, but he was happy to see the paraprofessional taking an interest in a severely disabled student.

Marks' first thought – that Fenster's actions were odd – was correct. According to court documents, Fenster took Juan out of the room and pumped him for information.

A teacher in a room near the hall where Fenster questioned the boy testified in court that Fenster repeatedly asked Juan, "Did he hit you? He hit you, didn't he? Where did he hit you?"

Juan's disabilities had left him uncoordinated, and he routinely bumped into desks and walls. It was not abnormal for the boy to have three or four bruises at a time. A week before the incident, Juan had bumped the corner of a desk and a large, dark bruise was visible on the outside of his left leg, just below the cuff of his shorts.

"Did he hit you here?" Fenster asked the boy. "Mr. Marks hit you on the leg, didn't he?" Finally, after questioning Juan for five minutes, the boy agreed Marks had hit him on the leg. Fenster then took the boy to the nurse's station, then to Principal White.

Fenster made an abuse report and had Juan show Principal White where Marks had struck him. White was familiar with the false allegations Juan habitually made and was skeptical. Seeing the doubt on Principal White's face, Fenster further alleged that she had witnessed Marks strike the boy. White was still skeptical but had to investigate the incident.

White believed that Marks could not have struck Juan without the students and teacher in the next room hearing the incident. Principal White did not want to question the special education Students, afraid that their testimony would not be reliable if the incident ever went to trial. White questioned the students and teachers in the next room.

Because of the partition, they had not seen Marks strike Juan, but they all said that they'd heard a clap and then crying. Because Fenster claimed to have witnessed the incident and witnesses claimed to have heard it, White was forced to report the incident to police.

Police officers came to the school and questioned Fenster and the students to whom Principal White had spoken. After getting the statements, the officers interviewed Marks. When asked about the incident, Marks told the police officer that the whole incident was a misunderstanding. Marks explained that he had clapped Juan's hands together, and he contradicted Fenster's written statement that she had been in the room at the time.

Because the boy was telling the same story Fenster was, and many students claimed to have heard the sound of Marks striking Juan, the police recommended charges be filed against Marks. The Arapahoe District Attorney agreed with the Aurora police detectives and filed charges of harassment by physical contact, third degree assault and child abuse against Marks.

After charges were officially filed, Marks was placed on suspension, with pay, pending the outcome of the legal proceedings against him.

"I was a member of the CEA," Marks said. "I wouldn't set foot inside a classroom without their protection. I immediately called the CEA for representation."

Greg Lawler was assigned to the case and immediately began an investigation, which is his first priority when handling abuse cases.

Lawler's Investigation

To prepare for trial, Lawler hired an investigator to determine the exact timeline of events. Lawler discovered that the timeline his investigator outlined did not match Fenster's timeline.

"Fenster claimed that she took Juan directly to the nurse's office," Lawler explained. "What we discovered was that over an hour elapsed between the time Fenster questioned the boy in the hall to the time she took him to the nurse's office. Once at the nurse's office, she continued questioning Juan. The nurse on duty stated she heard the questioning and that Juan was only giving her yes and no answers. Then Fenster took the boy to the principal. Once again, when the principal asked Juan questions, he only answered yes or no. Juan's one word responses became significant after my investigator questioned the boy's parents."

Karla Messmer, Lawler's investigator, interviewed Juan's father, Diego Mendoza, on March 18, 2001. The written transcript of the interview showed that Mr. Mendoza believed his son had not been abused.

"Mr. Mendoza explained that he had never been interviewed by anyone associated with the school or law enforcement," Lawler's investigator wrote. "Mr. Mendoza seemed to resent that he had been bypassed and ignored."

Mr. Mendoza then explained the history of the family's relationship with Marks and the reasons he believed Marks was innocent of all charges.

According to Messmer's report, Marks had met Juan's grandmother at a local laundromat. She and Marks had a conversation about her grandson, Juan, who was attending Badger Elementary School at the time. The grandmother was impressed with Marks and the family moved the boy to Laughlin Elementary School specifically for the reason that Marks was teaching the special education students there.

"We saw a big difference in my son. He was doing a lot better," Mr. Mendoza told Messmer. "After Marks was suspended, Juan became very stubborn for a while. Marks would never intend to harm or hurt Juan. He's a good teacher for Juan, and we still believe this is so."

Mr. Mendoza explained that his son cries when he's startled. According to Mr. Mendoza, Marks must have startled Juan when he clapped his hands together. Mr. Mendoza again stated that he did not believe Marks had struck his son. The father attributed the abuse accusation against Marks to Juan's poor English skills.

"I know that often Juan does not understand the question and he'll just say 'yes' or 'no' without really knowing what the question is," Messmer quoted Mr. Mendoza as saying.

The investigator then explained to Mr. Mendoza how Fenster had taken Marks to the nurse's office and asked the boy about a bruise on his leg.

"There are bruises all over my son," Mr. Mendoza told Messmer. "He and his brothers jump off of the living room windowsill, over the couch and onto the floor. My son has too much energy."

When asked what he and his wife wanted to see happen in this situation, Mr. Mendoza answered, "We want to see Mr. Marks back at the school and teaching my son again. He is a very good teacher for Juan. My wife told the principal that Marks is the best teacher my son ever had. We don't want him to lose his teaching license."

Lawler's investigator then interviewed a paraprofessional at Marks' school, Jill Waterston. Similar to Mr. Mendoza, Waterston had not been interviewed previously. Because she had not been contacted for a statement, Waterston called the CEA to speak with someone. Lawler tried to arrange an interview quickly but was hampered by the school district.

"The school district denied Waterston time off for anything relating to Marks' legal proceedings," Lawler said. "They advised her it was in her best interest not to get involved. My investigator finally had to interview her at a Denny's across the street from Laughlin over her lunch break."

Waterston was asked by Lawler's investigator to describe Marks as a teacher.

"He is a good teacher," Waterston answered. "He had a lot of stress because of Fenster and two other paraprofessionals, Erica Jones and Barbara Ayers. They did not cooperate with him. Fenster was the leader against Marks. She complained a lot. For the past eight years, Fenster decided which kids she would work with and refused to work with certain kids, regardless of what Marks wanted.

"Marks did things differently than the other teachers before him. Marks was open to ideas and suggestions from the paraprofessionals. In May 2000, I complained to Marks about Fenster's remarks about a boy, Brennan, having surgery. Fenster didn't like the kid. The boy would drool and Fenster would push him away from her in disgust.

"She would regularly complain to anyone who would listen about why these kids were born. She thought they should have been aborted because it would have saved taxpayers and the parents a lot of time and money. I finally complained to Marks about this because Fenster made many remarks like this, and I was concerned that she might hurt a child."

Marks held a meeting with the paraprofessionals following the revelation by Waterston which Fenster did not attend.

"All of us agreed that Fenster was nasty, and we didn't like her comments," Waterston continued. "We all agreed that Fenster had a negative attitude toward the kids. That group, without Marks, went to the principal to complain. Fenster was there for that meeting. Marks thought he could help her attitude without disciplinary action, though. At the meeting, Fenster said that I had misunderstood her, and the principal wrote it off as poor communication. I knew exactly what she meant because she was always making comments like that."

The investigator then asked Waterston about the reasons behind Fenster's dislike of Marks.

"It's not because he's a man or because he's gay," Waterston answered to the investigators surprise. "Fenster complained Marks was not like the teacher we had before him. I overheard Fenster's two paraprofessional friends discuss that now would be a good time to get rid of Marks. I think Fenster, as their leader, took it upon herself to accomplish that goal.

"At a seminar for paraprofessionals a couple weeks before the complaint, a paraprofessional from another school told the group about a teacher who had been dismissed for abuse. I think that story gave Fenster the idea."

Waterston explained that there were no shortages of bruises on Juan to bolster an abuse accusation.

"Juan throws himself on the floor and walks into things," Waterston explained. "He always had bruises. It wasn't hard to find a bruise on him and make it look like Juan had been abused. He can't understand the accusations he's making and is easy to coach because of that. This entire thing was a lie. Fenster was packing Mark's desk up the day he was suspended. She was ecstatic."

Waterston went on to state that Fenster had all but admitted to fabricating the allegation.

"She said that if she had known she could get Juan to say that Marks hurt him, she would have taught that to Juan earlier."

When Lawler read Messmer's report, he immediately forwarded a copy to the District Attorney.

"They ignored it," Lawler said. "Because they still had a room full of witnesses that heard the incident and Fenster claimed to have witnessed the abuse, the prosecutor still believed they had a case worthy of a trial."

The Trial

"The case against Marks was a 'he said-she said' proposition," Lawler said. "To clear my client's name, I had to discredit Fenster. The disgruntled paraprofessional claimed to have witnessed the incident, but from Marks' statement, I knew that was impossible. When a person is lying, they don't tell the same story every time. To trip her up, I got the statement she gave to the police and memorized every detail of it. I then waited for her direct examination at trial, knowing that the proof I needed would eventually come from her own mouth."

Lawler was anxious to proceed to trial. He believed that the faster the proceedings went, the quicker Marks would be returned to the classroom. However, the case would not be heard for almost another two years.

"We drew a judge that could not handle his docket," Lawler explained. "Routinely, Marks' case was the fourth or fifth case on the docket. Because of the way the judge handled his courtroom, he could only squeeze in about three cases a day."

To Lawler's increasing frustration, the case was continued six times.

"All six continuances were because of the judge," Lawler said. "However, he credited me for one, which still upsets me. I was five minutes late to court one day, when we were fourth on the docket. The judge never took the bench on time, but that day he did. My client was there and told the judge I would be present in several minutes, but he ordered a delay anyway. Because the judge charged the continuance to me, he was able to effectively circumvent my client's right to a speedy trial."

Because of the continuances and delays, the case did not proceed to trial until April, 2002. The morning of the first day was dedicated to sorting out the various pre-trial motions Lawler had filed. The prosecutor had not filed any motions.

Lawler used the motions hearing to begin laying the groundwork to discredit Fenster. The paraprofessional took the stand on a motion regarding the scope of her testimony.

The prosecutor walked Fenster through the events that had led to the abuse complaint. Unlike her statements in the police report, Fenster was now claiming she only heard Marks strike Juan.

"She had probably heard about our interview with Waterston and was changing her testimony," Lawler said. "I didn't pounce on her. I let her keep talking. The more she talked, the more fuel I had for trial."

Following the motions hearing, the court took a lunch break. In the afternoon session, the jury was brought in and the trial started.

The prosecution called Fenster to the stand first. Her testimony was the same as it had been in the motions hearing. After an hour-long direct examination, Lawler cross-examined Fenster. This time, he did not let the inconsistencies in her story go unchallenged.

"First, I challenged her statement to the police that she had witnessed the slap," Lawler said. "She tried to back pedal and say that she hadn't claimed to have witnessed it. I then produced her first signed statement, the police report and the school's incident report."

"Are the police officers and principal lying now?" Lawler asked her. "Or were you lying then?"

Fenster again claimed that her earlier statements were a misunderstanding.

"There seem to be a lot of misunderstandings," Lawler said. "Maybe we should walk through them one by one."

Fenster's eyes fell to the floor, and she did not reply.

"Let's start off with a statement you made earlier," Lawler said. "You claimed that you never made the abortion comment."

"That's correct."

"Would you be surprised to learn that I have four statements, one from each of the paraprofessionals you worked with, that say you did?"

"No," Fenster said. "You probably got them to lie for you."

"Now, your friends, the police and the principal are lying?"

"Yes."

"In your direct examination, you said that two other paraprofessionals, Jones and Ayers, had witnessed Marks strike Juan," Lawler said. "Are they lying again in every report when they said that they heard a clap but did not see the incident?"

"Probably."

"All right then," Lawler said. "Your testimony is that everyone is lying. That's what you're telling this jury, isn't it?"

"I guess so."

Lawler finished his cross-examination. The prosecutor then called the school nurse and the principal who testified about the bruise. Following their testimony, the defense rested.

Even though Marks did not legally have to testify, Lawler called him to the stand.

"I wanted the jury to see what my client was like for themselves," Lawler said. "From the way he conducted himself, the jurors saw that he was a caring, sensitive teacher. I had enough for a directed verdict, but Marks added a face to my case. The jurors could identify with him."

Following Mark's testimony, the defense rested. The judge then read the jury instructions aloud and the jury was sent to deliberate. Less than an hour later, the jury came back with a verdict – not guilty on all counts.

The Aftermath

Following the acquittal, Marks was free to return to the classroom.

During his two-year suspension, Marks and his friend had opened a floral arrangement shop in Denver. By the time he was acquitted, the shop was flourishing. Marks was happy where he was in his life, and he didn't feel like dealing with the ill feelings his re-entry to the classroom would have stirred up in both himself and the community. He is still running the shop.

Fenster was not disciplined for her false accusation and was never prosecuted for perjury. She still works as a paraprofessional in Colorado.

"Disciplinary action needed to be taken," Lawler said. "It's bad when a student makes a false accusation, but it's even worse when an adult does it. The adult fully understands the repercussions."

Lawler and Marks contemplated a civil suit against the district but decided against it.

"Marks had spent two years in and out of courtrooms," Lawler said. "By the time he was acquitted, Marks was ready to move on with his life. He didn't want to drag things out any longer."

Chapter 6

Kurt Apple

The Beginning

Kurt Apple had not planned for a career as a teacher. He only obtained a teaching license as an alternate in case he was not able to pay the bills as a writer. After graduating from the University of Colorado with a degree in English, Apple moved into his parents' sprawling house in the affluent subdivision of Boulder, Colorado.

He began writing the "Great American Novel" – certain he would soon obtain a publishing contract that would allow him to write books for the rest of his life. Apple envisioned a picture of his fair skinned, freckled face and lanky body gracing the back of a book jacket.

Apple's parents were supportive of his chosen career. They allowed him to live in the studio apartment above their garage, rent free, so he could focus all of his time and energy on his writing. Apple worked diligently and finished his first novel six months after he sat down to write it.

When Apple had the manuscript polished to perfection, he sent query letters and sample chapters to agents and publishers. While he waited for the publishing world to affirm his talent, he began writing his second novel. Apple waited three months to hear back from the publishers and agents. When the responses finally came, they were a huge blow to his ego.

Every response was a rejection. Most were form letters thanking him for the submission but stating that the manuscript "wasn't right" for the particular agency. A few offered honest assessments of the work. Those were especially difficult for the young writer. A New York based agent wrote that Apple's work "…did not rise above the level of its own earnestness." Another wrote that Apple's characters and dialogue "…did not set the work apart from a novel the average seventh grader would find beneath them."

Apple's parents worried that the struggling writer would never earn enough money to leave the family nest and that they would be forced to support their son for the rest of his natural life.

Apple's father voiced his concerns to his son and suggested it was time Apple found employment. Apple's father advised his son to use his teaching certificate. Apple was reluctant at first but figured he could use the three-month summer break to pursue his publishing dreams. Apple applied for a vacancy with Boulder Public Schools and received a job teaching fifth graders.

At the age of 23, he took the job, expecting to dislike teaching. But, after his first year of work, Apple couldn't imagine a more fulfilling job. He grew to care about his students and saw the job of teaching young kids as a noble calling. Apple used his first summer break to finish his second novel and submitted it to the same agents that had rejected him earlier. At writing conferences, he'd heard the need for patience and perseverance preached by every published author who lectured at the seminars. Apple still hoped to be a published writer but knew that he would continue teaching even if he received a large advance from a publisher.

Summer vacation ended without any responses from the literary agents, and Apple prepared for his second school year. By the end of the fall semester, Apple had again received rejection letters from every agent he had solicited. He didn't feel the disappointment he had experienced with the unanimous rejection of his first novel. Teaching children had caused Apple to re-evaluate his priorities. He'd come to realize that he'd been writing to become rich, which would allow him to continue in the lifestyle that his parents had raised him in. Apple no longer viewed the attainment of riches as a necessity. He now valued his role as a teacher above worldly wealth.

By the end of the spring semester, Apple's teaching career would become contentious and his happiness morph into a deep feeling of frustration. Apple could not have imagined that what seemed like a harmless disciplinary action would result in a legal battle that would reach the Colorado Court of Appeals.

Broken Hearts and Dreams

Looking back on the legal mess in which he became embroiled, Apple laughs at the irony of the day everything started. The heart of his legal issues originated on Valentine's Day, 1998.

As a grade school student, he'd hated the holiday. He hadn't been a popular child, and he'd watched other students give each other Valentine's Day cards while he received Valentines only from his parents and his teachers. As an adult, Apple wanted to spare the unpopular students in his class the feeling of isolation he'd experienced as a child on Valentine's Day.

At his request, Apple's students brought in old Kleenex boxes and he walked them through a craft exercise to make the boxes into Valentine's Day mailboxes. The students decorated their boxes with red and pink paint, paper hearts and glitter. He informed his class that their task was to place a Valentine in every box, without the recipient of the card seeing them.

For the students that couldn't afford to buy cards for the entire class, Apple bought a variety of Valentine's cards featuring different cartoon characters. By making sure he had an assortment of cards, Apple hoped the students couldn't tell which of their peers were unable to afford to buy their classmates cards. The students all seemed happy with the exercise and worked diligently on the boxes and their cards.

After the boxes were completed, Apple made sure the students had time to place their cards in the decorated boxes. Apple planned for the class to open their Valentine's mailboxes during a class party scheduled for the final period of the day. The party was always the last event because parents would bring in cookies and other sweets and the children would be bouncing off the walls, making further classes a waste of time.

His students' excitement and anticipation for the coming party built. The excitement peaked during the class before the party. Apple tried to drone through a lecture over nouns and verbs, but the students weren't focused. Sensing the lack of progress, Apple abandoned his lesson plans for the rest of the day. He opted to read to the students from the Harry Potter book the class had been enjoying. The students seemed to settle down as he read the story, save one girl in the back row of the classroom. Every time Apple looked up from the book, Amanda Lewis was leaning back in her chair and gossiping to the girl next to her, Katie Holden.

Apple stopped reading from the book three different times to remind Lewis of the "four on the floor" rule he had instituted for his students' safety. Each time, Lewis complied.

When he looked up and saw Lewis's chair legs up a fourth time, Apple made a fateful decision.

He stopped reading, put the book down and walked toward Lewis. The girl looked him squarely in the eyes. Apple met the girl's stare and gestured toward the floor. Lewis looked at him defiantly and continued reclining. Apple gestured again and the girl smirked at him, entertained by her new game. Apple threatened Lewis with losing her Valentine's Day party privileges, but the girl still refused to obey the chair rule.

Frustrated, Apple reached for Lewis's chair, intending to push the front legs of it onto the floor. Lewis, startled by Apple's sudden movement, reacted by leaning back farther to avoid the teacher's grasp. Lewis's movement was enough to unbalance her tilted chair. Her arms flailed wildly and she fell backward.

Everything began to happen in slow motion for Apple. He later reported that he experienced the next events from outside his body, hovering above the room as he watched the girl fall to the floor. Apple saw himself reach for Lewis. He sensed, more than felt, his hand interlock with her wrist. The playful look in Lewis's eyes had dissipated and was replaced by unmitigated fear. What took a split-second seemed like an eternity to the shocked and detached teacher. Apple lost his grip on the girl. When he lost his hold on Lewis's small hand, her momentum was irrevocably altered and the chair tilted up onto one of its back legs. Lewis tried to right the chair by shifting her weight, but her efforts only made the situation worse. The precariously balanced chair careened sideways, sending the frightened girl to the floor.

Apple watched in shock as Lewis's body fell, and the floor seemed to rush up to her. Apple watched, helpless, as Lewis's arm hit the floor, absorbing her full weight and force of the fall. Apple blinked rapidly as he regained his faculties. Slowly, he became aware of a long, plaintive wail, emanating from Lewis's small body.

Apple bent down to pick up the girl who held her arm as she winced in pain. He'd been trained in first aid and knew not to move the girl. Apple barked a command at Lewis's friend, Katie Holden, to get the school nurse. The girl stood frozen in place, her eyes fixated on her injured friend. Apple yelled for Holden's attention, and she snapped out of her trance. He told her again to get the nurse, and the girl finally ran from the room to the school nurse's office.

Holden found Nurse Yancey Claiborne in her office. Claiborne saw the look of fear on the young girl's face and knew something was seriously wrong. Claiborne quickly followed Holden to Apple's classroom. Once there, she could not see Lewis through the crowd of students circled around the injured girl.

Claiborne gently moved the students aside and bent over Lewis. Claiborne later testified that she instantly saw that Lewis was injured. Claiborne had brought an ice bag along with her and pressed it gently to Lewis's arm. The girl's lips trembled, and tears welled in her eyes.

Nurse Claiborne was more worried about the injured girl than the circumstances that caused the broken arm. She didn't ask Apple or his students what had happened. Instead, she notified the office that Lewis would need to be taken to the hospital immediately. The school's secretary, Theresa Warner, called Lewis's parents and they were at the school within minutes. Apple and his boss, Principal John Savage, walked next to the girl as she was taken from the building and loaded into the parent's waiting car.

As the parents drove away, the other children's parents were beginning to arrive for the school party. Savage told Apple to attend the party and reassure the frightened children. Savage informed Apple that he needed to call Lewis's parents and would get an incident report from the teacher after the parents were out of the building.

Apple went back to his class and tried to keep a calm appearance. He hadn't been teaching long, but he'd already come to realize that the students took their emotional cues from him. He facilitated the party, and the children seemed to put the Lewis injury behind them. Apple was amazed how resilient his students were.

After the party, Apple skipped cleaning up and went directly to Savage's office. Warner informed Apple that Savage was making his school rounds, but had left instructions to have Apple wait in his office. Apple did as he was instructed. While he waited, he began to mentally review the events of that afternoon, and he began to process the reality of the situation. With his realization came a knot of fear in his stomach. Even though Lewis's broken arm had been an accident, he was sure there would be repercussions.

The First Punishment

Apple had to wait over thirty minutes for the principal. When Savage finally arrived, he gently closed the door behind him and sat behind his large faux oak desk. Savage leaned forward and stared Apple in the eyes.

"Excuse the language, but what in the hell happened?" Principal Savage asked after a long pause.

Apple swallowed hard, then relayed the events that led to Lewis's broken arm to his boss. Savage listened quietly, but shook his head at Apple's description of trying to put the girl's chair legs on the ground.

"We gave you training on what is appropriate contact with a student," Principal Savage said. "You clearly crossed the line. Now, we have a girl with a broken arm, and we're probably looking at a civil suit. I can't let this slide. If you aren't disciplined, that can be used in court. I don't have many options here."

Apple told Savage he understood and offered without any argument to let a written reprimand be placed in his file. Principal Savage shook his head negatively.

"That's not good enough," Savage said. "I'm placing you on suspension, with pay, pending an investigation. I'm also required to notify the police. Additionally, I am sending the findings of my investigation to the Boulder Public School's Board of Education for resolution."

Apple started to reply, but Savage cut him off with a wave of his hand.

"These are serious accusations," Principal Savage informed Apple. "Don't say anything else until you consult an attorney. The police department will be in contact with you in the next few days. Don't waste any time in obtaining counsel."

Apple nodded his understanding, then stood up and shook Savage's hand. He then walked quietly from the office and the school.

The embattled teacher went home and informed his parents of the suspension. Apple explained to his father that he would probably need to defend against a criminal charge as well as a civil suit. Apple asked his father to retain the family's attorney for his defense, but his father had other ideas. Apple's father explained to his son that an attorney who specialized in defending teachers was required, but he offered to call the family's attorney for a recommendation. Apple's father called the attorney immediately, and he recommended that Apple contact the CEA for representation. Apple called the CEA that evening, expecting to get the teacher's union voice mail. To his surprise, Lawler was working late that night and he answered the phone.

"The first conversation I had with Apple was fairly rapid," Lawler said. "He was upset and nervous, and he spoke very quickly. I had to ask him to repeat himself numerous times. After hearing Apple's side of the story, I told him I didn't think criminal charges would be filed, assuming the students that witnessed the incident told the same story he did. However, I told him he was looking at a dismissal. I advised him that since the incident was an accident we could request a hearing to get him reinstated."

The next day, the Boulder Police Department requested an interview with Apple. Apple and Lawler went to the police station and gave a written statement.

"Following my client's statement, the police interviewed the students in Apple's class. Every student told the investigators that the incident had been an accident," Lawler said.

Despite the students' statements, assault charges were filed against Apple in March, 1998. The charge was a misdemeanor offense, and Apple wasn't arrested. For Lawler, the case was not complex.

"Apple disciplined a student in the course of his duties," Lawler said. "No one claimed he injured Lewis's arm on purpose. All of Apple's students, including Lewis, were telling the same story. For me, the prosecution didn't have much of a legal case. Based on the Chapel Legislation, I believed Apple was immune from criminal liability. On the day of the trial, I submitted a motion to dismiss."

The Boulder County Court magistrate ruled in Apple's favor and dismissed the charges.

"The judge ruled that Apple's conduct in regard to the student making the allegation was reasonable, that he had acted within the scope of his employment, and within the discipline code promulgated by the school board, pursuant to the Chapel Legislation. He was therefore immune from criminal liability. The court then dismissed the charges against Apple."

The Boulder School Board had not terminated Apple's contract prior to the trial. Because Colorado law provides that a teacher convicted of a crime is automatically terminated, the school district hoped to spare the expense of a termination hearing. Following the dismissal of criminal charges, the school board was forced to act.

School Board Meets

The Boulder School Board met in May, 1999, and, based on the Lewis incident, elected not to renew Apple's teaching contract for the 1998-99 school year. Apple was notified of the board's decision near the end of the month.

"Apple was a probationary teacher since he'd only been teaching for two years," Lawler said. "Until a teacher is non-probationary and entitled to due process, his contract is year to year. By opting not to renew his contract, the school board was once again trying to circumvent a termination hearing. I wasn't going to let it go at that. I subsequently filed a mandamus action against the school district."

A mandamus action asks a court to enforce the statutory provisions of legislation affecting teachers that states that a teacher or any other person who acts in good faith and complies with the discipline code adopted by a board of education shall not have his or her contract non-renewed because of such lawful actions.

Lawler and Apple had to wait until November, 1998, for their action to be heard in court. Before arguments could begin, the school district filed a motion for dismissal. The school board argued that

Lawler's motion for a mandamus action "failed to meet the requirements for the extraordinary remedy of mandamus."

The judge took the matter under advisement. The next day, the school district's motion for dismissal was granted.

"I thought the ruling was inappropriate," Lawler said. "Apple's case met all requirements of the law, but the judge didn't apply the law the way it was intended. The legal threshold the judge used was so high, almost every mandamus action would be dismissed. The judge wanted the mandamus action to meet specific, technical statutes that conflicted with the school district's adopted disciplinary code. I really had no choice; I couldn't let that ruling stand. It would have affected every teacher facing dismissal in the state. Sharon Dreyer stepped in at that time to pursue the appellate process with me. We filed an appeal with the Colorado Court of Appeals less than a month after the lower court's ruling."

Lawler and Dreyer filed the appeal in January, 1999. Because of numerous motions by the district requesting more time, oral arguments would not be heard until December, 1999.

"The school district was stalling," Lawler said. "They argued over legal fees they were liable for under Colorado law, which took months to resolve. They argued that the case law we cited in our filing was a new argument to them and that they weren't prepared to argue those legal issues without warning. The extra time the district obtained allowed them to concoct a second legal argument. As well as claiming that a mandamus action wasn't warranted based on the facts of the case, they also argued that the remedy we sought was moot.

"Now, the school district was arguing that they did not renew Apple's contract not only for the Lewis incident but also for budgetary reasons. They stated part of the reason they weren't renewing the contract was that the school district couldn't afford Apple's salary. That was laughable. The school district could afford to pay six figures to appeal but couldn't afford a twenty-eight thousand dollar salary."

Colorado Court of Appeals

While he waited for his appeal to be heard, Apple resumed writing. He poured his anger and frustration into several short stories which were published in national magazines. He also began to rewrite his two previous novels. Apple hoped that by placing his personal experiences and emotions into his characters, he could make the stories more believable. He also contracted with a New York based freelance agent to edit and review his books.

Despite the forward momentum in his writing career, Apple's first goal was to return to the classroom. He knew that he had the talent to be a writer but the calling to be a teacher. Apple's teaching career was still in its infancy, but he believed he could grow into the type of teacher that could influence children for the rest of their lives. To help him achieve that goal, Lawler called in Sharon Dreyer to assist with the appeal.

In December, 1999, Apple was present at the courthouse as Dreyer gave oral arguments in front of the Colorado Court of Appeals. Apple was fascinated by the experience. The judges entered the room, were seated, and arguments began.

Dreyer addressed the court first. After the green light on her podium was turned on, Dreyer explained the need for mandamus in Apple's case and explained why she thought the lower court was in error. Dreyer anticipated the district's budgetary argument and claimed that any dismissal action, for whatever the school district's stated reason, stemmed from the Lewis incident. Dreyer also argued that Apple had followed school district's discipline guidelines and despite his probationary status was immune from dismissal. Dreyer further stated that her motion for mandamus should not have to meet strict, technical guidelines to be heard. As she was concluding her statement, the green light on the podium switched to red.

Dreyer's time for oral argument was finished. She thought it odd that the judges had not interrupted her with their own questions. Generally, the judges interrupt arguing counsel frequently with questions about the broad implications their ruling would have. Appeals of other cases to the court would be impacted by their ruling. The appeals court judges also had to worry about a potential appeal to the Colorado Supreme Court. As a matter of ego, no judge likes to have his or her ruling overturned by another court. By not asking any questions, the judges were likely signaling to

Dreyer that they had already ascertained the legal ramifications of their potential legal finding.

As Dreyer and Lawler pondered the judges' behavior, the attorney from the school district, David Lester, received a green light to begin arguments.

The judges interrupted Lester before he could finish the sentence "May it please the court," which is the ceremonial opening for oral arguments. The judges wanted to know what he believed the legal standard should be when a mandamus action is filed. Lester answered by citing the Colorado statute that governs the criteria for mandamus relief to be granted. According to Lester, the Colorado statute provides for mandamus relief only if, "The plaintiff has a clear right to the relief sought, the defendant had a clear duty to perform the act requested and no other remedy was available."

Lester then argued Apple's request for mandamus failed to meet any of the criteria.

"Mr. Apple does not have a clear right to the relief sought because of his probationary status," Lester said. "His clear duty was to provide for his student's safety. His actions were contradictory to that duty, and they resulted in an injured arm. Lastly, Mr. Apple was granted a termination hearing which satisfied the requirement for additional remedies. The fact those remedies failed is not a basis for a mandamus remedy."

Lester asserted that the school district could legally dismiss Apple for cause but that the school district had non-renewed the contract for budgetary reasons.

"School budgetary reasons for dismissal do not warrant mandamus," Lester said. "The remedy sought is only appropriate if the non-renewal of the teaching contract is a result of disciplinary measures. The school district should be able to non-renew a contract for financial reasons without judicial oversight."

To bolster his argument, Lester stated that because the non-renewal was not based on the Lewis incident, the school board did not have to give Apple a hearing.

Lester was interrupted numerous times. He barely had enough time to finish his arguments before the light on his podium turned red.

Lawler tried not to read into the judges' questioning of Lester.

"The judges may have had legal questions that they needed answered to issue a ruling which they felt couldn't be appropriately addressed by Dreyer," Lawler said. "I don't think the questions tipped their hand. The judges were just being thorough. However, I thought we had the stronger legal argument. It was just a matter of waiting to see if the judges agreed with me."

The Colorado Court of Appeals ruled on the case within three months. In March, 2000, the court ruled in Apple's favor.

The appeals court found invalid the school district's argument, that Apple could be terminated for the Lewis incident. In their published decision, the majority opinion stated, "Colorado statute prohibits school boards from basing decisions not to renew probationary teachers' contracts on actions taken both in good faith and in compliance with the boards' discipline codes. Here we find that the school district's actions were not in compliance with the law."

The court also rejected the school district's claim that Apple could be let go for budgetary reasons.

"The school board argues that mandamus relief is inappropriate because another avenue of relief exists to remedy any violation of statute," the court wrote in the majority opinion. "According to the school board, its determination of the reason for nonrenewal of a contract does not constitute an abuse of discretion. We disagree. Mandamus is an appropriate remedy when an agency ignores or violates statutory restrictions on its authority."

Dreyer's final argument, that the lower court's ruling used an inappropriate standard, was also addressed in the opinion.

"We disagree with the school board's argument that the teacher's complaint failed to state adequately a claim upon which mandamus relief could be granted. When viewing a motion to dismiss, a court must accept as true the allegation of the complaint, under any theory of law, and decide if the plaintiff is entitled to relief. The complaint provided sufficient notice to the school board of the facts and theory underlying the teacher's cause of action."

The Colorado Court of Appeal's ruling reversed the lower court's ruling. The case was sent back to the lower court to hear the mandamus action.

"The appeals court only decides the issue before it," Lawler explained. "They couldn't issue a ruling on mandamus, but they could force the hearing."

The lower court entertained oral arguments on May, 2000. Lawler and Dreyer argued that their client's actions followed discipline guidelines. Unable to claim budgetary reasons for the dismissal, the district argued only that they had non-renewed the contract for cause. The judge found in Apple's favor.

Apple returned to the classroom for the 2001 school year but at another school district. Despite his experiences, he is not bitter about the legal proceedings.

"He saw the legal system work," Lawler said. "I believe he walked away with a faith in the legal system many people don't have. He tries to convey his feelings to his students. In a way, the entire incident was positive for him. Apple believes he's a better teacher and writer as a result of his experiences.

Apple still uses his summer vacations to continue his writing career. He's sold several more short stories but is still trying to publish his first novel.

Chapter 7
Jack Ericksen

The Beginning

Jack Ericksen grabbed the calf's legs and pulled. Slowly the baby slid from its mother's womb and stood shakily on its legs. The veterinarian couldn't remember how many calves he'd birthed since he began practicing in 1965, but the sight of a newborn struggling to walk still astounded him. As Ericksen watched the newborn stand shakily on its legs and walk over the blanket of snow that covered the Aspen ranch, his cell phone rang. A Carbondale City Council member was calling him regarding a zoning issue.

In addition to his thriving country veterinarian practice, Ericksen was the mayor of Carbondale – a small mountain town situated along the western slope of Colorado. Ericksen was an outspoken advocate for the city of Carbondale and the Roaring Fork Valley. The affluent mountain town of Aspen was only a ten-minute drive from his home, and the ranches that bordered the town gave him a lot of business. Ericksen also taught veterinarian tech classes at Colorado Mountain College where he'd been a professor for twenty-two years. Because of the calf's birth, Ericksen was late for that evening's class and hurried through his conversation with the councilman.

Ericksen hurriedly drove to the junior college. His class was eagerly waiting for him. Ericksen threw his belongings on his desk with an audible thump and immediately launched into his lecture. As he spoke, his students took furious notes. Ericksen held a doctorate degree in Veterinarian Medicine and had completed post-doctorate work in both veterinarian surgery and anesthesiology. Ericksen's students respected him for both his education and real life experience and they enjoyed listening to his lectures. The vet's speaking skills and reputation were two of the reasons he was routinely re-elected to office.

After he finished his lecture, students raised their arms in the air to ask him questions. Like his jobs, the questions were varied. Several students asked him about the techniques on which he'd just expounded, and student Wendy Miller asked him about the affects of Colorado's on-going drought on the city of Carbondale.

Water conservation was a favorite subject for Ericksen. His political platform had been based on the need to conserve water. Ericksen gave his students several ways they could help save water. Among the things he listed was not flushing tampons down the toilet. Ericksen explained how the feminine hygiene product clogged toilets and sewers, causing water to backup and overflow. Every student except Miller bobbed his or her head in agreement.

Wendy Miller was one of Ericksen's laziest students. She was often ill prepared for class and her homework assignments were rarely completed on time. Ericksen had told Miller numerous times in the past that if she didn't care more about her work, she should find another profession.

Since then, Miller had increasingly become argumentative and combative in class. Ericksen could see that Miller was looking to pick another fight, but he did not have the energy to deal with it. Before Miller could say anything, Ericksen told the class that he was exhausted and that class was over for the day.

Miller slammed her hands on the desk in front of her to express her frustration, but followed her classmates out of the room without incident.

Ericksen did not have time to worry about the young woman's frustration. He had two committee meetings to attend that evening, as well as a house call to a local ranch to put down a lame horse. He'd be lucky if he saw his wife and two kids before midnight.

The Complaint

Two days went by, and Ericksen forgot about Miller's growing hostility. Following an appointment in Aspen for a sick cow, Ericksen drove to the college. Before he could make it to the classroom, Dean Sandy Giovanni stopped him. Giovanni told Ericksen that she needed to speak with him immediately. Judging from the

Dean's tone of voice, Ericksen knew that whatever news his boss had was not positive.

Giovanni led Ericksen to her office and closed the door behind them.

"We've had a complaint of sexual harassment," Giovanni said without any formalities. "This college has a zero-tolerance policy for such behavior. I'm suspending you without pay pending the outcome of an investigation."

"What exactly was I supposed to have done?" Ericksen asked. "I need more information."

"Several female students are alleging that you offended them in class by using sexually explicit comments about tampons in the sewer system and that you regularly make jokes about blondes, feces and other things that aren't appropriate in a classroom setting. Because your 1991 suspension is still on your record, I'm asking the College Board to non-renew your contract."

Ericksen immediately knew who had lodged the complaint. He shook his head in frustration and left the office without comment. Ericksen called the CEA for representation. Attorney Brad James was assigned to the case. Greg Lawler joined Ericksen's legal team after the college termination hearing.

"Most people think that the CEA protects only K-12 teachers," James said. "The CEA actually protects every teacher in the state, including college professors at public colleges. Issues at colleges come up less frequently than at lower level schools, but professors are still vulnerable. Ericksen is one of only a few college professors that the CEA has defended over the years, but his case was the most memorable.

"The charges involved in Ericksen's case were outrageous, and the end result of all the legal proceedings was very dramatic. Considering Ericksen's reputation, it's difficult to understand how things progressed as far as they did. Ericksen was the Mayor of Carbondale, a long-time veterinarian, and he'd been teaching at the college since 1973. Any reasonable person would have looked at the situation and resolved it without disciplinary action. However, once I talked to my client and got the background on the situation, I understood what the college's administrators were up to."

During Ericksen's tenure at Colorado Mountain College, he'd had a profound influence over the Vet Tech program. Ericksen, like many long-time teachers, began to protect the program as if it was his own child.

During the fifteen years before Ericksen's second suspension in 1995, the college had experienced a decline in student enrollment and suffered budget cuts. Prior to the decline in student enrollment, Ericksen had been the head of the Vet Tech program. In 1983, the college needed to cut programs and staff. Colorado Mountain College abolished Ericksen's position and cut numerous academic programs. They also mainstreamed their operations by closing a satellite campus. Ericksen continued to serve as the de facto head of the Vet Tech program, despite not being financially compensated for his leadership role.

Ericksen's relationship with some of the other faculty members at Colorado Mountain College became strained in 1991. Despite the college's budget cuts, Ericksen used his influence as a practicing veterinarian and the mayor of Carbondale to have a new Vet Tech building erected off campus.

"After that, Ericksen's colleagues resented him," Lawler said. "He also had a run-in with two incompetent teachers that deepened the growing resentment of Ericksen and his program."

Micah Winters and Ellen Whitt held Associates degrees in Animal Care and taught several lower-level courses in the Vet Tech program. Ericksen was bothered that the two women were paid as full-time employees despite the fact that the women taught only part-time. With the college's strained budget, Ericksen perceived the salaries of the two women as inappropriate. The women consistently received poor student evaluations and formal faculty evaluations each time they were reviewed.

"Both women were incompetent," Lawler said. "Winters did not teach students how to convert from standard to the metric system because she did not understand it herself. That conversion is extremely important when administering drug dosage amounts given in milligrams. Whitt refused to teach the students about animals she didn't like, especially llamas. In a mountain community, llamas are an important and widely used animal."

As the de facto head of the program, Ericksen believed Winters and Whitt were hurting the education of the students in the program, and he recommended their termination. To save their jobs, the two women retaliated with a sexual harassment complaint against Ericksen in 1991. The complaint lead to his first suspension.

At the time of the 1991 suspension, Giovanni was a professor on the College Board. Ericksen approached Giovanni about the allegations, but Giovanni refused to speak with him because she was counseling Winters and Whitt.

"The 1991 suspension was handled improperly," James said. "The peer review committee that heard Ericksen's grievance in relation to his 1991 suspension found numerous problems with the manner in which the investigation of the allegation was carried out and the manner in which Colorado Mountain College interpreted its own sexual harassment policy, in particular with the way in which students were contacted and questioned by Giovanni."

Ericksen believed that the suspension was due in part to the actions he took in protecting the Vet Tech program. He may have been a politician, but Ericksen wasn't a diplomat. He was a salt-of-the-earth type guy, comfortable kneeling in the muck of a working ranch to tend to an injured animal. Ericksen's job contributed to his crusty and demanding personality. When he fought with the administration, it was often adversarial in nature. He was the clichéd "thorn in the side" of the administration.

In March of 1993, Ericksen was reinstated after nine months without pay. He immediately faced another complaint and was given a reprimand. The peer committee issued their finding and a recommendation in June 1994. The committee found that Ericksen had acted appropriately and that the reprimand should be withdrawn. Ericksen was never notified that the college had cleared him.

In 1995, Winters and Whitt were still teaching but harbored ill feelings toward Ericksen. The two women sought out students prior to their mid-term for a "reduced stress" meeting. Court records showed that the women were actually trying to get students to make a complaint against Ericksen. Wendy Miller attended the meeting. Days later, she lodged her complaint.

Months prior to the formal complaint by Miller, the college went through a leadership change. Giovanni took over as Dean of the college and gained supervisory powers over Ericksen. Upon assuming her duties, Giovanni immediately ordered a review of the Vet Tech program. Giovanni had no background in veterinarian medicine and held only a Bachelor's Degree in Liberal Arts. The new dean and Ericksen were quickly at odds. Giovanni had maintained her relationship with Winters and Whitt. As the friction between Giovanni and Ericksen grew, Giovanni used the two women to monitor Ericksen.

"Ericksen received excellent formal evaluations every year in which he was observed and evaluated by Colorado Mountain College administrators. He also received excellent student evaluations every year. The college was looking for a reason to get rid of him, and Giovanni seized the opportunity of the complaint she helped manufacture to get rid of Ericksen."

James' Investigation

James began looking into the allegations following his conversation with Ericksen.

"I called the school expecting to resolve the issue, but Dean Giovanni told me right off the bat that she was recommending Ericksen's termination." James said. "She informed me that another female student had substantiated Miller's claims and that the college had a zero-tolerance policy on sexual harassment. I tried to explain to her the context of Ericksen's comments, but Giovanni said that it made no difference. I knew there had been friction in the past between them, but Giovanni's blatant hostility towards Ericksen surprised me."

Following his conversation with Dean Giovanni, James called Ericksen to tell him to prepare for a legal battle.

"I told him we'd wait until the termination was official and then decide on the best course of action. There was no way we'd let the termination go uncontested."

Colorado Mountain College has a four-part grievance and dismissal policy with four levels of review: an informal meeting between the grievant and his or her immediate supervisor; a full hearing before a faculty peer review committee; review by the College president or designee; and a review by the Colorado Mountain College Board of Trustees. Under this policy, the board's decision is final. James defended Ericksen in the hearing before the peer review committee, on which Giovanni was a member.

The Hearing

The hearing began with the complaining woman, Wendy Miller, testifying. Miller claimed that Ericksen's comment had been degrading, not because of the context of the comment but for the tone of Ericksen's voice.

"Miller was claiming the way Ericksen said the word 'tampon' made it sound dirty and vulgar. Her complaint was not that Ericksen brought it up in class. She was alleging that his voice inflection made the comment a form of sexual harassment," James said.

Miller further testified that Ericksen routinely wandered off the topic of his lecture, such as the time he brought up John Elway in class and that he used crass words and terms in his lectures on biological matters. Miller stated that Ericksen used multiple terms for feces such as "big chair," "big dog" and "floaters and sinkers."

"The comments looked bad when they were taken out of context," James said. "The comment about John Elway came when the Broncos' quarterback was injured. The class was talking about it, and Ericksen made an off-hand remark. The comments about feces came from a lecture in which he was using real-life experiences and examples from the CDC to explain the topic of diseases carried by human and animal waste. Ericksen described the cases he was involved with on a daily basis and categorized them. He was a blunt professor who worked in the field all day. The comments were not meant to be vulgar or crass. They were actually meant to lighten a topic that might be unpleasant for many people. He used these terms with people that wanted to work in the veterinarian field. If they can't handle talk of feces in a lecture, how were they going to handle it in real life?"

James cross-examined Miller and asked her why the comments offended her. She answered that the subject matter was uncomfortable for her. James then asked what type of grades Miller received, and the woman admitted that she was a below-average student.

James ended his cross-examination and Miller's corroborating witnesses were called to the stand.

"They all testified that Ericksen had made the comments," James said. "We agreed that he said them, but I tried to get them to testify to the context of the comments during cross-examination. Every student admitted that the comments were appropriate for the situation in which they were said."

James then called Ericksen to testify. The professor explained his comments in their context. Following his testimony, the defense rested.

"We proved several things in that hearing," James said. "Most importantly, we showed that Ericksen hadn't sexually harassed Miller. We also showed that Miller made the complaint for all students in the class, but she wasn't speaking for everyone. Most of the students believed that the comments were appropriate. Based on the testimony of the hearing, I expected a reinstatement, but I was wrong. I hadn't accounted for two variables.

"Three years before formal complaints against Ericksen were filed, the college had dealt with another sexual harassment complaint against a different professor. The college had taken no action and had been disciplined by the state. The college was ultra-sensitive to sexual harassment allegations and was determined to take action. The fact that Giovanni and two teachers in the Vet Tech program disliked Ericksen made getting rid of him a palatable solution. The College Board recommended his immediate termination. Giovanni then upheld the termination and the Trustees followed her lead."

The Civil Suit

James disagreed with the opinion, but his options to fight the ruling were limited.

"We needed to find a way to have his case heard within the legal system," James said. "Although the state courts were an option, I began looking at this case from a federal level. After reviewing cases with similar fact patterns, I discovered that the First Amendment Rights afforded Ericksen under the United States Constitution protected his speech in the classroom. The two teachers who had complained about Ericksen were teaching the course and were using his notes. The use of the notes demonstrated that the entire sexual harassment charge had been formulated simply to oust him. The federal courts could not force the college to re-instate Ericksen, but they could financially penalize the school district for wrongful termination. The best course of action was to sue the college on the grounds that they violated Ericksen's Constitutional Right to Free Speech."

James spent most of the next year drafting his legal filing for the Federal District Court with the help of Lawler. Lawler and James had a long history together prior to the Ericksen case. James had clerked for Lawler while in law school. Because Lawler had experience in First Amendment, James relied on his mentor's experience.

"The civil suit I filed on behalf of Ericksen was based on the fact that his termination constituted a violation of his First Amendment rights," James said. "The comments he made were allowed in his employment contract with the school. By terminating my client for those comments, the school had stripped him of his right to free speech."

To win in a civil suit, James had to meet several standards. He needed to demonstrate that Ericksen's comments were within the scope of his teaching contract, which was predicated upon the college's guidelines for conduct, including sexual harassment. The two other requirements were to show that Ericksen's comments were justified in the context they were made and that the content of the remarks was based on the assigned material of the class – material that the college had approved and was still using.

The college's guidelines for a professor's conduct concerning sexual harassment were defined in the employee handbook Ericksen received at the start of every class year. The college defined sexual harassment as…"Participation in fostering a work or educational environment that is generally intimidating, hostile or offensive because of unwelcome or unwanted sexually-oriented conversation, suggestions, requests, demands, physical contacts, or attention or displays of sexually-oriented pictures, drawings, calendars or jokes."

Colorado Mountain College's defined sexual harassment policy formed the cornerstone of James' legal argument.

"To say that Ericksen's comments violated that policy, the school would have to abandon the entire Vet Technician program," James said. "It is impossible to discuss medical issues without delving into the biological functions necessary for life. Students who chose that field must consider discussions of basic health issues as a matter of course. Miller was overly sensitive and should not have been in that program. Based on the college's own policy, Ericksen's actions were relevant to the teaching material and necessary for the discussion. Therefore, his comments were not unnecessary or unwanted and should not have been viewed as sexual harassment."

James filed the civil lawsuit mid-November, 1997, but the case did not proceed to trial until late-September, 1998. Attorneys for Colorado Mountain College elected to have the case tried in front of a jury as opposed to being heard by a judge in a bench trial.

"I started by having my client testify to his comments and explain their context," James said. "I then called students that had been in his class to testify about those comments. Every person testified that his remarks had been appropriate."

Next, James and Lawler used witnesses to explain the friction with the school.

"Through those witnesses I demonstrated that Ericksen's battles with administrators in relation to the college's budget cuts and staffing issues. Every witness testified that his relationship with the college had been tense."

Because one reason the college listed for Ericksen's termination was his feces comments, James called an expert witness to explain Ericksen's terms such as 'floater and sinker'. Dr. Cynthia Merit had been a professor in the Vet Tech program at the college for seventeen years.

"Is there ever a time you need to discuss the fecal matter and its appearance?" James asked.

"All the time," Merit answered. "If you have a situation where you've got an animal that has loose or dry stool you have to be able to describe it to the vet on hand. That helps them with the diagnosis of what is happening to the animal. The fat content of the stool causes it to float or sink and tells the vet what the animal has eaten.

To help the students understand, Dr. Ericksen and I both bring the topic back to humans. Thus, the terms he used were actually to explain the feces in a way that students can remember."

"What have you done as a teacher during [the time of Ericksen's suspension] to adjust your teaching to increasing sensitivity?" James asked.

"I've avoided a lot of things that I would have talked about in the 1980s," Merit said. "I've actually changed my curriculum because it is too dangerous. The terminology used can bring up complaints of sexual harassment. Human examples have always been used in class to help with the learning and now everyone is scared to, even if not teaching the material negatively affects the students' ability to work in the field."

James and Lawler rested their case and the attorneys for Colorado Mountain College presented their defense.

Miller was the first witness they called. During her direct examination Miller asserted that Ericksen made inappropriate comments, including blonde jokes and that his use of the word tampon had been designed to embarrass the female students of the class.

Lawler cross-examined Miller.

"In your deposition, you wrote that Dr. Ericksen used tangential information to help you remember information and that you appreciated the information from a veterinarian and that Dr. Ericksen should not be fired. Is that still your position?"

"I think what he said was gross and shouldn't have been said."

"Can you give me an example?"

"The issue with the tampon."

"Can you tell me what was said before the tampon comment?"

"No," Miller admitted. "I hadn't been paying attention before that."

"But you can tell us what he said after that?"

"Yes. I started paying attention then."

"Your classmates testified that the comment was about Dr. Ericksen being in a sewer and seeing something that looked like a rat. After he picked it up, he realized it was a tampon. Would they be incorrect?"

"I wouldn't know."

"What did he say after that?"

"Dr. Ericksen was telling us not to flush tampons down the toilet."

"And you took that as sexual."

"It was gross. I was offended."

"When did you decide to make a complaint?"

"Soon after that."

"Was that after the 'stress reduction' meeting held by Ms. Winters and Ms. Whitt?"

"Yes."

"What about that meeting prompted you to file a complaint?"

"Ms. Winters gave us examples of things to complain about and what to be aware of. She told us what to do if we heard Dr. Ericksen say anything like that."

"She told you to look for something to file a complaint about?"

"Yes."

Lawler expected Dean Giovanni to testify next, but the Dean never took the stand. Instead, the college's lawyers began focusing on the college's termination procedures.

"They tried to assert that the college was justified in terminating Ericksen because he had been given warnings in the past," Lawler said. "The problem with their argument was that my client had asked for clarification as to how to explain sensitive subject matter to students without causing complaints and the college administrators told him there was nothing they could do.

"Through Miller's cross-examination, I demonstrated that administrators did know how he could protect himself, but they wanted to leave him vulnerable. The college's administrators were in essence setting him up. They knew that Ericksen could not discuss the material he needed to teach his course without getting a complaint at some point. They had been waiting for that complaint and when it came, they terminated him."

Following their witnesses, the defense rested and the case moved to closing arguments. The college summed up their case, asserting that Ericksen had sexually harassed students and that Colorado Mountain College was justified in terminating him.

During his closing argument, Lawler immediately attacked the college's evidence.

"The college's case is smoke and mirrors," Lawler began. "The college has anonymous, unsigned, unsupported documentation. Go ahead, we don't mind if you see their evidence – but bring it to the stand. Empty chairs is what we had in their case.

"It's time to pull down this paper curtain. They have some paperwork saying things happened, but they didn't bring it to the stand. And that's their responsibility. In America, that's how we try cases. You can make allegations against a person, but when a jury is going to make a determination, bring the witnesses to the stand so both sides can talk to them. Where are the blonde jokes? Where are the dirty jokes? Where's the vulgarity? Where? It's nowhere but in that paper trail, in that paper curtain, and it's time to pull it down."

Next, Lawler called into question the credibility of the witnesses against Ericksen.

"If you're going to make a sexual harassment claim, bring me a victim," Lawler said. "Not one witness in this 1995 case came in here and said 'I was sexually harassed.' It's smoke and mirrors. When asked the questions directly and pointedly, they said no sexual harassment occurred. We brought our case. No sexual harassment occurred in 1995. And isn't it amazing that the administrator who listened to all of the evidence in this case comes in and says, 'Yeah, he violated the sexual harassment policies,' when no one, no one said it happened."

Lawler then tied the college's termination of Ericksen to the First Amendment.

"Enough is enough," Lawler bellowed. "This is First Amendment versus politically correct. And if politically correct has gone so far as to take an individual student out of class, the lowest common denominator – and I call her the lowest common denominator, I don't care what grades she got, they can get A's or B's. The school used one person against a class of twenty-six people to come in here and talk about how she was offended.

"Who gets to chose in a classroom whether Dr. Ericksen uses the word feces or big dog or stool or anything else to talk about the subject matter? Is it the lowest common denominator? Is it a student with an ax to grind against this doctor? Or is it the doctor who knows this material? "If you're going to gag a professor like that, we might as well start burning books because that's what [the college is] doing."

Lawler's voice was rising and he began to approach the jury box. The judge had strict rules regarding the conduct at attorneys, and he pointed a finger at Lawler.

"Counsel, stand at the podium," the judge ordered sternly. "And keep it down."

Lawler apologized and resumed attacking Colorado Mountain College's case.

"I think the First Amendment has extraordinary value to this democracy, and I think that it is important for the free-flow of thought, for the free-flow of ideas for communication, to allow professors to be open, to move amongst their class. When I sat there and listened to how Dr. Ericksen was ultimately locked in front of his television screen, putting notes on the board, I realized how he had been gagged. It's not just his First Amendment, it's all of our First Amendments, and we can't let it slip."

Lawler then rested and the judge prepared to hand the case to the jury for deliberations. However, the college's attorneys asked for a directed verdict.

"The motion was denied and the case went to the jury," Lawler explained. "We were asking for over a half-million dollars, which is essentially the money Ericksen would lose over the remaining years of his career. I expected the jury to take a while to reach their verdict and was a little nervous. The issues that the jury was looking at were somewhat complex."

Lawler's nervousness grew when he and James received a message stating that the jury had a question for the judge.

"Juries often need some testimony read back to them or they have a legal question for the judge. Questions can indicate the direction in which the jury is leaning. I was anxious to hear their question."

That afternoon, the jury's question was read aloud in court.

"The jury was asking the judge if they could exceed the amount we were asking for," Lawler said. "I've never had a jury ask that before. It didn't take a rocket scientist to know what the jury was thinking. The judge instructed the jury that they could not find additional damages beyond what Ericksen was asking for."

"Does that mean they're finding against the college?" Colorado Mountain College's attorney asked in a stunned voice.

The judge informed the defense counsel that the question was a legal point and not to read into it. However, Lawler and James knew the case had been won. Neither attorney spoke during the reading of the jury's question.

Five minutes later, the jury returned with their verdict. They'd found that the college had violated Ericksen's First Amendment rights and unlawfully terminated him. The amount they awarded surprised Lawler.

"They awarded $557,100," Lawler said. "The jury clearly saw through the school's lies and saw that they created the situation that they used to terminate Ericksen."

Colorado Mountain College immediately appealed the ruling. The appeals process lasted until 1999, and the appeals courts upheld the jury's decision.

"During the appeal process, interest was piling up on the initial judgment," Lawler said. "When all was said and done, Ericksen walked away with close to a million dollars between the award, attorney's fees and interest."

Following the judgment, Ericksen returned to his duties as mayor of Carbondale and to this day continues his veterinary practice.

Guilty Until Proven Innocent

Chapter 8
The Uncertainty Principle

The Theory

In 1927, physicist Joseph Heisenberg conceived of and wrote the Uncertainty Principle, a physics theory that states a scientist cannot take measure of something without affecting it. Heisenberg intended his theory to apply only to scientists conducting experiments. The physicist reasoned that the methodology a researcher used in an experiment must be factored into the results.

For example, in order to measure a beam of light, a scientist would bombard the light beam with a laser. Because the beam of light has absorbent properties, the laser alters it during the experiment. The researcher gauging the results must factor in the effect energy from the laser had on the results of the experiment to determine how much reality was affected by the methodology.

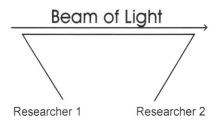

The Uncertainty Principle was intended for use only in scientific experiments, but it can be applied to everyday situations, such as the media's coverage of luminous or high-profile trials. Taken out of its original context, the theory becomes a paradigm of social science theory.

The paradigm for the new application mirrors the experiment

used to measure light. By labeling the light beam being measured as the court case, the researcher using the laser as the media and the researcher looking at the altered reality as the public, it is possible to show how media impacts the public's perception of a case, and

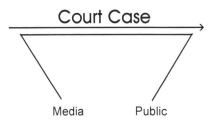

by correlation, the jury pool.

Changing Communications

Methods of communication have changed throughout the course of American history. During the Salem Witch Trials, local news and opinions were broadcast through the pulpits of American churches. This method of sharing information and ideas was filtered through Puritan dogma. The Puritans believed in the personification of evil, and preachers viewed changes in the society as the results of an evil influence.

The main source of social change in early America came from the newly immigrated Quakers. The Puritan preachers' sermons created mistrust between the two religious groups which eventually gave birth to a mass hysteria over witchcraft. The fact that Quakers were the sole targets of witchcraft allegations was a direct result of the theology that was espoused in the local churches.

Allegations of witchcraft were kept local because the sermons and newspapers of the time were not shared between towns. This kept the panic confined to the Salem, Massachusetts, area. As the methods of communication changed, so did the ability to spread influential ideas and destroy reputations.

Newspapers of the time were printed with the intention of keeping an individual town's historical records. With the advent of the mail system, newspapers became a method of communicating between towns, but the medium's reach was still confined to a small area. Eventually, radio and television were invented which allowed for communication on a national scale. With each invention came a watershed trial that demonstrated the power of the ever-changing media.

Trial Applications

In 1865, John Wilkes Booth, an actor, assassinated President Abraham Lincoln. Booth's actions that night created a controversial set of circumstances that led to Dr. Samuel Mudd's conviction for aiding in Booth's escape and conspiracy to commit murder.

Dr. Mudd was drawn into the historical episode because Booth sustained a broken leg after he jumped from the President's box to the stage below. Despite the injury, Booth ran to a waiting stallion and fled the state. The assassin eventually made his way to a barn in Maryland. A local man, not knowing of the assassination, found the injured Booth and sent for a doctor. Dr. Mudd lived a mile from the barn and came to offer his assistance. Dr. Mudd set the leg and treated Booth for a fever. Booth recovered and continued to flee from authorities.

The next week, the law caught up to Booth. He was executed on the spot for his crime. Since Dr. Mudd's treatment had enabled Booth to continue his flight from justice, Dr. Mudd was charged with aiding in the escape. A charge for conspiracy in the planning of the assassination was added later.

Dr. Mudd was tried in a military tribunal created by President Johnson who succeeded Lincoln. Only one witness testified in the tribunal against Dr. Mudd. The man who had initially summoned Dr. Mudd for help claimed the doctor conversed with Booth in whispers. The man testified he believed the two men had known each other previously.

Despite no other physical evidence, Dr. Mudd was convicted. Journals of the jurors, examined by historians, showed the jury had been swayed by print reports of the crime depicting Dr. Mudd as a planner of the assassination and a southern sympathizer. Dr. Mudd was later pardoned, but his conviction was never overturned. Dr. Mudd's descendants are still trying to clear his name.

Almost fifty years later, Bruno Hauptman was tried and convicted for the kidnapping and murder of the Charles Lindbergh baby. Hauptman, a German immigrant, worked as a handy man for the Lindbergh family. After the Lindbergh's baby became missing and was found dead, Hauptman was arrested and executed for the crime. Newspapers and radio stations across the nation covered the events and the trial.

Hauptman's German heritage was reported exhaustively. The crime had taken place in post WWI America, and Germans were seen as the enemy. Because Hauptman was German and Lindbergh was an American, the murder was covered as an attack on an American hero.

Hauptman had an alibi, but he was portrayed by the media at the time as a liar. The most damning piece of evidence against him was a wooden ladder. Hauptman's own ladder was said to match the type of wood fragments left on the ground under the baby's window. Hauptman was convicted and executed based on that evidence. Modern forensics has proven that the slivers of wood actually did not match Hauptman's ladder.

Hauptman has not been officially cleared of the crime. Speculation now centers on other workers in the Lindbergh home. To date, no concrete evidence of guilt has been uncovered.

Modern day examples of the Uncertainty Principle include the Orenthal James Simpson trial. Because of extensive media coverage of the case, the trial was moved to Los Angeles County. Had the trial remained where it was originally set to be heard, a jury of his peers – affluent Americans – would have tried Simpson.

Instead, the jury was comprised of middle and lower class Americans. The jury pool allowed Simpson's defense to prey on that community's mistrust of white police officers. Simpson was acquitted by jury nullification. Ironically, the media coverage that facilitated the change of venue has left the former football great shunned by the public.

The law has been unable to keep up with the fast-paced changes to American technology. Instant communication is now possible which allows the media to cover court cases in ways that the men who drafted the Constitution never imagined. The First Amendment of the Constitution, which guarantees freedom of the press, now clashes with the accused's Fourth Amendment right to a fair trial.

The responsibility for eliminating potential bias now falls to the media. Due to the creation of twenty-four hour cable news networks, the competition for advertising dollars is intense. The networks need high-profile trials, such as Simpson's, to attract viewers. The media's shift from an emphasis on journalism to maximize profits lessens their ability to completely remove themselves and their opinions of the case from the coverage of actual events.

Commentators and legal analysts now cover the cases. The commentators, such as Bill O'Reilly of the Fox News Network, are encouraged to share their unfettered opinions with the American public. The blending of opinion and news broadens the impact of the media's coverage and increases the media's impact on the reality of the case. The first commandment of journalism to be impartial keepers of the nation's history, modern-day scribes, has been abandoned.

Media Pressure and Errors

In college, future journalists are taught to be objective. All personal biases need to be set aside when covering a story. However, reporters are members of society, and their approaches to stories reflect society's values, as well as their own.

In an era that has seen the advent of the Internet, television, facsimile machines and cellular phones, journalists are under increasing pressure to get a story out quickly. A delay of only minutes now leads to a news agency being scooped, which results in a loss of advertising dollars. Because of the need for speedy reporting, facts are not checked thoroughly, and there is inadequate time to edit out phrases that display a personal feeling.

Stories about people in a position of trust abusing children are the clearest example of how reporters' biases seep into their coverage. Reports of Catholic priests molesting young parishioners and allegations of teachers physically and sexually abusing students fill modern headlines. The stories are sensational not only for their salacious content but for the societal anger they engender. Reporters are not immune to feelings of revulsion about the crimes and their word choices reflect their personal disdain for the supposed crimes.

Whether intentional or not, stories about abused children contain numerous phrases that indicate bias. The effect the statements have are increased or mitigated by the story's placement in the paper. Stories printed on the front page of the newspaper or placed near the beginning of a newscast are more likely to be viewed, which gives the inflammatory phrases more power. The further back a story appears, the less impact it has on the society which comprises the jury pool that will sit in judgment of the accused.

Inflammatory Words

The phrases used to describe the accused and their alleged crimes are often innocuous but, viewed in the full context of the story, can take on skeptical or sarcastic tones and imply guilt. Because of journalistic style, several phrases appear consistently, in the same order.

Reporters write in 'Inverted Pyramid Style,' a method that gives the *who, what and where* first. The rest of the story is dedi-

Inverted Pyramid Style

How	Conclusion
Why	Body of Article
What	Next Several Paragraphs
Who/Where	Lead Paragraph

cated to the how. This style allows editors to cut words for space without losing necessary facts.

When discussing a suspect prior to conviction, newspapers use the word alleged to describe the suspect and his possible crime. As a result of Inverted Pyramid Style, the story's first line often reads, "*John Doe, a local middle school teacher, allegedly abused students.*"

The word *alleged* should convey a lack of judgment, but in

the modern press, based on the way reporters use the word, it indicates guilt. This is because the word *alleged* is used only in conjunction with the suspect's actions, not the victim's statements. It is also used when a defense attorney offers an alibi or statement that shows innocence. By using the word for one party only, the word *alleged* places a higher degree of credibility on the victim's statement and fosters the public's mistrust of the accused.

Alleged is the most common inflammatory word, but news stories contain several others. Following the paragraph naming the suspect and his crimes, news stories also contain interviews with officials from the school district.

As a matter of policy, school districts suspend a teacher accused of abuse. Because of the policy, the school district is in the process of suspending the teacher when approached about the story. The suspension is then reported because of the allegation. This gives the supposed charges more credence because the suspension is not explained as a legal necessity.

Following the interviews with district officials readers will usually find an explanation of the events that led to criminal charges, interviews with the parents of the victims and the community's reaction. The word *concern* is featured prominently. The teacher's actions are reported as a concern to the district and community despite the fact that the charges have not been proven.

"The reporter asks for comments from the community before all of the facts are known," Lawler said. "Community leaders comment on what they've been told by the police and prosecutors, not the facts. As the Colin Quinn case demonstrated, a prosecutor can use the time before trial for public relations. By giving negative community statements early on, community leaders play into the prosecution's public relations plan. Often, the teachers are beloved by the community. In order to get a conviction, prosecutors need to strip the defendant of all of his credibility. Reporters have to know they're being used to advance a case, but regardless, they report events the same way every time."

After reporting on the alleged crime and getting community reaction, the accused is offered a chance to comment by the newspaper or television station. When introducing quotes made by the defense attorney or accused, the word *embattled* often appears.

Embattled gives the public the impression the accused is under siege, which detract from the veracity of the accused's statements. The defense statements are viewed as defensive posturing by an accused suspect under fire from law enforcement officials.

"No matter what we say, because the word *embattled* appeared before it, we look like we're manufacturing a story to give us a fighting chance," Lawler said. "And that's assuming that I have something to say besides 'No comment.' You put the word *embattled* before a 'no comment,' and it looks like an admission of guilt."

The news stories conclude with, "*If convicted, John Doe faces ten years in prison.*"

"The reporter is giving an end to the story that may not be relevant," Lawler said. "He is assuming the natural progression of the charges filed is to a trial and conviction. There's still a chance the case will be dropped, settled or dismissed. By stating a teacher would get ten years if convicted, the reporter is assuming it's a case worthy of going to trial. Often the teacher is innocent, and the reporter is evaporating the most important belief in American jurisprudence – innocent until proven guilty. Instead, news accounts make it appear that an accused child abuser is *Guilty Until Proven Innocent.*"

Television stories follow a similar style, but the phrases used can be even more damaging than print reports because a television reporter's facial expressions are visible during his statements. A raised eyebrow, a smirk, an incredulous look or a change in voice tone can indicate skepticism or convey anger. Because a television report is live, it is impossible to edit out reporter's reactions.

In television, the video images that accompany the story also set a mood. Seeing a teacher on the ground in handcuffs, being led to a squad car or hiding his face in shame adds to a perception of guilt.

The accused and his attorney are in a precarious position if they agree to be interviewed for a national television story such as *Dateline NBC*. A television reporter is not necessarily looking for a good sound bite but a moment of pure reaction. During the interview, the reporter may warm up the subject with several easy questions. Once the accused is bantering with the reporter, a tough question is asked. If the accused looks surprised or stammers during his answer, that sound bite is used in the story. The result is an image of the accused fumbling to defend himself.

Another tactic television reporters use is to make a statement during the interview. The reporter stops during the statement and looks at the accused. Because the natural human tendency is to avoid silence, the interviewee tries to finish the statement. The subject then rambles through a long answer. The more the accused talks, the more likely he is to say something contradictory or open a line of questioning. The reporter pounces on the subject and the accused's look of shock or confusion is then edited into the piece.

One final tactic is for a reporter to ask the tough questions early. When the subject thinks the worst is over, the reporter then brings up a document or piece of evidence of which the accused wasn't aware. The look of surprise is again used in the story. Every example has the same effect. The subject's reaction leads to a loss of credibility.

Altered Reality and Outcomes

Due to the impact of the media coverage, the accused is left not only fighting the evidence but the mystique of the charges as well.

"When we begin the jury selection process, one of the first things we have to do is search for potential bias. We ask prospective jurors if they have read or seen any news coverage about the case, but even that isn't fool proof," Lawler said. "Even if they haven't been exposed to prejudicial coverage they may have talked to someone who was influenced by the media reports. You have to assume potential jurors come in with an altered reality of the case. Our job is to change that perception back to what actually happened."

Media saturation also presents another potential problem.

"In some cases, jurors will lie to get on a jury," Lawler said. "In high profile cases, the jurors can become temporarily famous themselves. There are financial reasons for a potential juror not to be completely candid during the jury selection process."

Lawler cites a Simpson jury member who later posed for *Playboy* as an example.

"She made money off her participation in the trial," Lawler said. "Tell me she didn't know the potential was there when she got her jury summons."

The defense counsel can ask questions to check for bias, but Lawler admits the process is imperfect.

"The Vois Dire process, the process of selecting a jury, is tough. Everyone has some level of exposure to the media. What I look for is someone who can set aside pre-conceived notions and just hear the evidence to reach a fair verdict."

The media manipulation does not stop once the trial begins.

"During a trial, evidence presented by the defense showing innocence is spun by the prosecution," Lawler said. "When a victim recants, he is depicted as scared or confused. The public is reminded the victims are children. Stories and editorials about the children being revictimized are published. That's one reason people don't like attorneys. It looks like we're picking on helpless students, not the vindictive conspirators we sometimes deal with."

During the trial, newspaper accounts of the story gradually

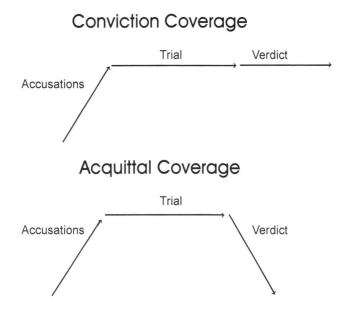

Conviction Coverage

Accusations • Trial • Verdict

Acquittal Coverage

Accusations • Trial • Verdict

begin to slip farther back into the paper.

"Trials can be long and technical," Lawler explains. "Most of the time there is not much to report. Occasionally, a juicy fact will be revealed in court, and the story will jump to the front page. For the most part, media attention lessens until the verdict."

Once the verdict is announced, the press either downplays it or makes it front-page news. Should a conviction result, the story is front-page news. Lawler has discovered his client's acquittals receive very little attention.

"Once my clients are judged not guilty, the stories are buried in the paper," Lawler said. "Their arrest was front page news. It doesn't balance out. The treatment the press gives an acquittal makes it tough for my clients to go back to their old lives. Their reputations are shattered, and the media sure isn't helping to put it back together."

When the acquittals are covered, the prosecution is given a chance to explain why it didn't obtain a conviction.

"In the story about the acquittal, the prosecutor is often quoted saying that my client got off on a technicality or the prosecutor explains how tough it is to get a conviction for an abuse case," Lawler said. "It's never that he lost because the accused was innocent. The general statement prosecutors give is that they were proud of their prosecution and they'd do it again. The public reads that, and they don't want that pervert teaching their kids. Even in a losing case, the prosecutors are able to take one more chunk of my clients' reputation."

Media Aftermath

After the trial, teachers found not guilty discover that their problems aren't over. The glare of the spotlight is gone, but the stigma of the charges remains.

"The media move on to other stories, but the impact never fades," Lawler said. "My clients try to reintegrate themselves into the community, but the community doesn't want them back. It's the equivalent of a scarlet letter. Once you're branded a molester, there's always going to be some doubt in the public's mind. They've read so many horrible things about my client they believe some of it has to be true. The teachers can leave the state, but with the Internet, the news reports are only a click away. The allegations will follow the teacher everywhere they go."

The residual effect of the media's impact is also evident when a teacher is reconsidered for reinstatement.

"The school district is under no obligation to reinstate a teacher," Lawler said. "The impact of the public's new perception of the teacher is considered by district officials. The officials are very reluctant to put a teacher back in the classroom for public relations reasons. They also fear a civil suit by the teacher. Reinstatement is an admission that the district was wrong."

Lawler has been forced to take legal action in order to reinstate the teacher in almost every case examined in *Guilty Until Proven Innocent*. School districts have admitted that their reasoning for keeping the teacher terminated or suspended included the community's outrage and negative news reports.

"The district fears a storm of bad publicity," Lawler said. "In some ways I can't blame them. The school's phones are ringing off the hook with calls from angry parents, and school officials have already been through a firestorm of publicity. However, the bottom line is, teachers wrongly accused should not be punished for crimes they did not commit.

"By not reinstating the teacher, the district is sending the wrong message to their impressionable young children. Students are seeing the justice system treated disrespectfully by authority figures. How can we expect those same children to respect the system when they become adults?"

Lawler also does not blame parents for voicing their anger to the school district.

"Parents' perception of the situation is that a pervert somehow got off on criminal charges and will be in daily contact with their children," Lawler said. "It's understandable when you look at the media coverage. Unless the parents sat through every day of the trial, they are going to believe the worst, because that's the way the media presented the teacher and the situation to the public."

Media Cases

The media's impact on trial cases will be examined over the next five chapters. The Carr and Wilder cases, outlined in the introduction, were driven by the media. In *Denver Post* news articles, both men's respective school districts blamed the media coverage for making it impossible to return the teachers to the classroom.

Aaron Marks spent two years in the media spotlight after he was accused of abuse. Two years into the case, it became clear that the alleged victim had lied. The case was dismissed, but Marks has not worked since.

Lori Salmon was never charged with an offense; but, due to media pressure, she was fired from her job. Salmon's only action to warrant the dismissal was to place a student in a locked side room when he got unruly. The media innacurately portrayed the incident as a teacher locking a student into a small supply closet.

Each case examined has one central theme. Each garnered local and sometimes national media attention. The paradigm outlined earlier in this chapter is applicable to all five cases. The first media reports were front-page news. Editorials were written about the allegations and community leaders were quoted voicing concerns. Once charges were filed, the prosecutors were interviewed routinely by the press. The trials were covered in-depth, but the acquittals received scant coverage.

By not fully covering the resolution of the cases, the media failed to correct the damage done by its measurements of the trials. The innocent teachers' names cannot be fully cleared without balanced coverage. This imbalance intensifies the lasting effect the negative media coverage has on the innocent teachers involved. In the final analysis, the media's scrutiny of the cases affected the public's perception of the accused and permanently altered the teacher's reality.

Chapter 9

Darren Carr

The Beginning

David Carr's heart broke. The twelve-year-old boy was sitting alone at the Washington Elementary School lunch table with no food in front of him. Carr had witnessed the same scene play out multiple times over the course of the school year. In the past, Pedro Lopez's mother had spent her state aid checks at the local bar. Carr assumed that her money had been misspent again, and her son would be without lunch money for the rest of the month.

Pedro sensed Carr's gaze and turned his thin body around until he faced the teacher. The boy's plaintive eyes locked onto his. Despite the boy's lack of facial expression, Carr could see a deep sadness lurking behind Pedro's big brown eyes.

Carr sighed and looked at his tray of food. He felt guilty eating when one of his students could not. Carr wondered if the boy would even eat a hot dinner that night. He was sure Pedro hadn't eaten breakfast. The boy had asked to eat an apple on Carr's desk during the first period of school that morning.

The tall, bearded and slightly balding teacher reached into his pocket. Carr was ten days away from payday and money was tight, but he could not afford to see his student starve. Carr found enough money in his pocket to buy another lunch. He bought a second lunch and walked to Pedro's table with the two trays of food.

Carr placed the small tray of food in front of Pedro and sat down across the table from him. Pedro thanked his teacher and then quickly devoured the meal. Not much was said between the two, but Carr expected that. Even when called on in class, Pedro's answers were a maximum of three words.

The boy finished his meal and said, "Thank you," then left the table for recess. As he walked away, Carr realized Pedro was wearing a tee shirt, torn and faded jeans, and he didn't have a coat. October is usually mild in Colorado, but the fall of 1989 had been particularly cold. Weather forecasters were calling for snow that night. Carr called after Pedro and offered the boy his coat. The proud boy simply shook his head negatively and kept walking.

The incident stuck in Carr's mind. Over the next several months, Carr brought an extra sandwich with his lunch for Pedro and gave him a coat at Christmas time. Carr knew he could do little more for Pedro. District guidelines did not clearly delineate teachers' responsibilities from those of the parents. Carr hoped to discuss the situation with the boy's mother, Guadalupe, but she never attended the school's parent-teacher conferences.

Carr continued to try to help Pedro, but no matter what he did, the sadness in the boy's eyes remained. As the school year ended, Carr wondered how the boy would manage throughout the long, hot summer in Bristol.

Pedro's Living Conditions

In March of 1990, Carr glimpsed the lifestyle to which Pedro had gone home every night and would be subjected to every moment of the summer.

Carr was leaving school at five in the evening and Pedro was still sitting on the sidewalk in front of the school. Seeing his student on school grounds so late, Carr was naturally curious.

He walked up to the boy and asked him why he was still at school. When Pedro shrugged his shoulders, the school secretary, who was sitting with the boy, answered for him. Pedro had missed his bus and gone to the school's office to call his mother. The school's secretary had called the mother, but there was no answer at the home number.

After trying for an hour, the secretary tried to call Ms. Lopez at work. She was informed Ms. Lopez had left work at three p.m., the same time school got out. The school had no information about Pedro's father on file, so the secretary called the home every thirty minutes. Carr asked Pedro why he didn't walk home and the boy answered with two words, "Too far." Feeling sorry for the boy, Carr offered Pedro a ride home. If he were lucky, Carr would finally be able to speak to the boy's mother.

The two drove in silence through the streets of Bristol. Pedro spoke only to tell Carr where to turn. The boy navigated Carr from the affluent end of town, past a set of railroad tracks that delineated the social classes of the small farm town, to a tiny two-bedroom house near the town limits. Pedro's house was more than five miles from the school.

Three children sat on the cracked curb in front of a home that was as cracked and faded as the sidewalk. Flecks of paint hung precariously to the sides of the dilapidated home and the structure seemed to be tilting sideways. Carr asked Pedro who the three children were, and the boy informed him they were his siblings.

Carr got out of his 1985 Nissan and approached the children. He asked if their mother was home, and like Pedro's speech pattern, their answer was brief. Carr learned the mother was inside sleeping.

Carr left Pedro on the curb with his brother and sisters and knocked loudly on the front door. When no one answered, he knocked again. Finally, Guadalupe Lopez opened the front door just enough to stick her head out. Her voice was hoarse and her eyes were bleary. Carr knew Ms. Lopez didn't speak English; her son was just learning the language. In fluent Spanish, Carr explained who he was to Ms. Lopez, and she opened the front door fully, and then stepped aside so he could enter.

Carr looked around the room. The inside of the house mirrored the decay of the exterior. Laundry and fast food wrappers littered the floor. Nothing was cooking on the stove. On the edge of the coffee table, a box of cereal lay on its side, the box's contents spilling onto the floor.

Despite the resentment towards the mother building in him, Carr tried to remain civil. He asked her if she needed help with Pedro, expecting the same proud rejection of help that came naturally to Pedro. Surprisingly, the woman shook her head affirmatively. She explained that she'd quit her job as a farm hand recently and had taken a job in another town. The cost of living was expensive where she was moving, and she needed to find a place for her son or he'd have to work in the fields with her.

Carr had heard that Guadalupe had a criminal record for solicitation. He assumed the mother had turned tricks just to feed her children. When Guadalupe explained to him that her son would be better off living with someone else for a short time, Carr didn't argue with her. Guadalupe asked Carr to take the boy but explained that she wanted Pedro back when she could better afford to take care of him. Despite a nagging voice in the back of his mind, Carr agreed to take care of Pedro.

Ms. Lopez thanked Carr and quickly packed her son's meager belongings. The faded tee shirt and jeans Pedro had always worn to school were about the only clothes the boy possessed. Among the other few possessions she packed was an old, leather baseball glove. Carr glanced down at Pedro's meager belongings and the voice in his head was quieted. Despite his worries about violating school district policy, Carr felt the arrangement was good. The boy needed someone to take care of him, and he had the means and resources to do it.

Carr took Pedro home with him that night. They pulled into his driveway at 10 p.m. Despite the late hour, Pedro explored Carr's home. The boy marveled at the size of Carr's average three-bedroom home. Pedro was too tired to sleep, and Carr didn't want to force the issue. Pedro needed time to adapt to his new surroundings.

The boy spent his first few hours inside Carr's home looking at pictures and asking questions. Carr didn't mind the endless questions; they constituted more communication from Pedro than at any time in the past. Pedro was especially curious about a picture showing Carr with his arm around a tall, blond woman.

Carr explained that the woman was Gale Norton, now the United States Energy Secretary. Carr had served as the district manager for Norton's 1990 senatorial campaign. Carr also explained he served on the Bristol City Council and as the chairman of the county Republican Committee. Carr explained to Pedro that he would be absent one night a week for meetings.

Pedro was most impressed by the amount of food in Carr's refrigerator. Carr had to suppress an urge to laugh. He hadn't bought groceries for over two weeks and by his standards, the fridge was empty. Pedro's reaction to his limited food reminded him that the boy hadn't eaten dinner, and Carr quickly fixed eggs and left over green chili for huevos rancheros. As he did with his school lunches, Pedro ate his late dinner quickly.

For the rest of Pedro's time there, Carr vowed to keep the refrigerator full. The boy needed to feel secure, and Carr could help the process by making sure Pedro never worried from where his next meal was coming.

After dinner, Carr showed Pedro the room that was to be his. Pedro looked at Carr's sparse guest bedroom and said, "Big." Carr nodded and explained to the boy that he'd fix it up. The next day, Carr bought posters of famous baseball players and baseball team pennants for the bedroom walls.

After the first night, the two settled into a comfortable routine. Carr would get up early and pack Pedro's lunch, then drive the two of them to school. The two would eat lunch together, and Carr would drive Pedro home in the evening. Once at home, they ate dinner. Pedro was assigned chores. Among those was cleaning the dishes. After dinner, Carr helped Pedro with his homework. When the boy finished, Carr would then read to him from a book they picked out together at the school library.

On weekends, Carr drove Pedro to Denver to watch the Zephyrs, the local semi-professional team. During their trips, Carr showed Pedro the state capital building, the Denver Mint and other local landmarks. When they didn't go out of town, Carr took Pedro to the local library. By spending time reading with the boy, Carr hoped to improve Pedro's grasp of the English language.

When summer break came, Pedro and Carr spent many hours at the local park. Along with buying him a new wardrobe, Carr had oiled Pedro's baseball glove and was teaching the boy to throw and catch. Ms. Lopez visited once during the three-month summer break, and Carr's heart ached for Pedro when she left without promising to return.

For a few days after her visit, Pedro regressed to one-word answers and the sadness Carr had noticed earlier returned to the boy's eyes. Carr doted on Pedro during that time, and eventually Pedro's eyes were filled with merriment and laughter.

The summer went fast and Carr found himself caring more

and more about Pedro. Carr enjoyed the time that the two spent together and began worrying about Pedro's eventual return to his mother. Carr considered asking Ms. Lopez for permission to adopt the boy but decided not to. He didn't want the fragile tie between Pedro and his mother to be completely severed. Pedro could experience psychological harm and feelings of complete abandonment if his mother was not involved, in some fashion, with the boy's life. Ironically, Carr's affection and care for the boy that precluded him from adopting Pedro would end his teaching career in Bristol.

The Allegation

The 1990-91 school year started. Pedro was now in the fifth grade. Because they were still at the same school, Carr kept daily tabs on Pedro. The boy's teachers found him bright and engaging. In a complete reversal from his days in Carr's class, Pedro had to be asked to raise his hand in class less to allow other students to participate and to limit his gregarious answers to a few sentences.

As Pedro's English improved, so did his social skills. Pedro made numerous friends, and Carr would occasionally use his planning period to watch Pedro playing touch football with them during recess. Carr was watching when the catalyst for his legal problems occurred.

In April, 1991, during a touch football game, Pedro jumped high in the air for a ball, lost his balance and came down awkwardly on his right arm. As Carr watched in shock, Pedro writhed on the ground and howled in pain.

Carr rushed to the boy's side. Tears filled Pedro's eyes, and he reached his good arm out for Carr's hand. Carr grabbed the boy's hand and held it. He instructed one of the other students to go and get the school nurse. The nurse came quickly. After examining Pedro, she assured Carr that nothing was broken but advised him to have Pedro's arm checked by a doctor.

Carr quickly arranged for a substitute to cover his class and drove Pedro to the hospital. Once there, the teacher was not able to see the boy. After they finished treating Pedro, the emergency room doctors couldn't release the boy to Carr because he didn't have custody or power of attorney. Instead, the boy's mother was called. It took her nearly four hours to reach the hospital. After ascertaining Pedro was uninjured, she released Pedro to Carr. Her visit lasted five minutes and she never said a word to Pedro. Further, Ms. Lopez did not have insurance and the boy wasn't covered under Carr's policy. Carr paid Pedro's bill out of his own pocket before leaving the hospital.

The incident made Carr aware of legal ramifications his care of Pedro had created. If a major emergency or decision occurred with Pedro, he did not have the legal authority to seek help. Carr determined to fix the problem and contacted Ms. Lopez to sign over power of attorney.

"I didn't want to take her custody rights away," Carr said. "I just needed to make sure I could properly take care of him. I wanted her involved in Pedro's life; I knew he'd be hurt if she wasn't. I just needed to make sure I could handle any emergency."

Ms. Lopez agreed to sign the paper and did. However, the legal action had severe consequences for her. Ms. Lopez had been receiving state aid for the fourteen months Pedro had resided with Carr. Once the power of attorney was filed, the state became aware that Pedro hadn't been living with his mother. Ms. Lopez's state aid was based on the number of children living in her house.

Because Pedro hadn't been there for fourteen months and the living arrangement hadn't been reported, she had collected state aid for him. Ms. Lopez was liable for the money she had wrongly collected, and the state began proceedings to reduce her aid and penalize her for non-compliance with the state's aid guidelines.

The loss of income was unanticipated by Ms. Lopez, and she became angry. Within a week of her written notice for aid reduction, Ms. Lopez filed papers with the Prowers County Court alleging Carr had tricked her into signing the power of attorney document. When the court threw out her motion, Ms. Lopez contacted Prowers County Social Services and made an allegation of sexual abuse against Carr. Under Colorado law, the state agency was required to investigate the incident.

The Evaluation

Carr and Pedro were referred by Prowers County Social Services to Haynes-Seaman, an unlicensed psychologist with the Kempe Center, who claimed to have the ability to ascertain whether abuse had taken place by analyzing the videotaped interviews of the alleged suspect and victim.

Haynes-Seaman published her controversial method in *Children Speak for Themselves*. The book explains that Haynes-Seaman's evaluation methodology relies on body language, as opposed to oral victim statements, to make a diagnosis. The psychology profession has not and does not condone her methods, but because she is unlicensed and does not claim to be a practicing psychologist, the State Medical Board cannot review her actions or take disciplinary action.

"Innocent people she diagnosed as abusers have attempted to sue her, but the state employee was untouchable in court as well. All civil cases were thrown out of court without being heard because state agencies are granted immunity. By diagnosing abuse cases for the state, immunity applied to her actions," Lawler said.

One of the lawsuits was detailed in Haynes-Seaman's book. In her book, the little girl is called Becky. Becky's grandmother started to suspect the girl's father of sexual abuse after the girl started asking her grandmother about 'Hiney Games.' The 65-year-old grandmother reported her suspicions to Arapahoe County Social Services. A resulting investigation was inconclusive.

Becky's mother and father divorced shortly thereafter. According to Haynes-Seaman's book, Becky came home with blood in her underpants after a visit with her father. A doctor's exam revealed the little girl's vaginal area had been penetrated. The doctor called social service, which then called Haynes-Seaman for an evaluation.

The grandmother accompanied the little girl to the evaluation. A week after the interview, before the girl or her grandmother saw a copy of the written evaluation, police officers, social services workers and Haynes-Seaman herself showed up at their door and took the little girl.

The girl was placed with her father who on the advice of Haynes-Seaman had pleaded "no contest" to a charge of exploitation of children relating to the possession of child pornography. Haynes-Seaman's evaluation had determined that the grandmother was the one abusing the child and that the elderly woman was conspiring to frame the girl's father.

Haynes-Seaman cited the girl's memory of spitting out beets and her body language told her that the grandmother was not recognizing her limits as a child and that the grandmother, who had been abused in the past, hated men.

She also took an innocent joke by the grandmother – "That's what mothers do...they live to make their children crazy." – as evidence of the 'pathological influence' the grandmother had over the child.

A court eventually returned custody to the grandmother, but Haynes-Seaman was still called on by Prowers County Social Services to evaluate possible abuse cases.

Carr visited Pedro during the time that the boy was undergoing videotaped interviews with Haynes-Seaman and her staff, unaware of the psychologist's history or methodology. Haynes-Seaman videotaped the interaction between Carr and Pedro. Then, Pedro was interviewed. The boy vigorously denied that Carr had done anything inappropriate to him.

Haynes-Seaman ignored Pedro's statements exonerating Carr and focused only on his body language. Pedro had been ripped from Carr's loving home and placed in a cold, sterile environment. The boy's posturing was defensive. Haynes-Seaman took that as a sign he had been abused, despite Pedro's statement. Haynes-Seaman's evaluation went further than diagnosing Pedro as a victim of abuse. Despite the fact she did not interview any other children or teachers, the psychologist determined that Carr had molested four other children and was part of a sex ring.

Haynes-Seaman's evaluation was sent to the Colorado Bureau of Investigation for a determination. The CBI investigated Carr, but found that Ms. Lopez's charges were false and stemmed only from a custody matter.

Despite the CBI's findings, the Bristol School District suspended Carr with pay, pending the outcome of his legal proceedings.

The Public Takes Notice

It was during this time that the case became public knowledge. Despite Carr's good intentions, the Hispanic community of Bristol was outraged. In letters to the editor, the Hispanic community complained that a white man was raising one of their children. They stated a belief that Carr could not properly teach Pedro about his heritage and culture. Despite the fact that Ms. Lopez had placed her son with Carr, they asserted that it was racist for a white man to raise a Hispanic child when Hispanic families were routinely turned down when they tried to adopt a white baby.

Ms. Lopez was quoted in the small town paper stating that Carr had stolen her son and that he had tricked her into signing power of attorney papers.

While the Hispanic community's outrage was voiced, Carr's legal troubles continued. Despite the CBI's findings, Prowers County convened a dependency and neglect hearing based on Ms. Lopez's allegations. Carr retained a local attorney and fought the charges.

The dependency and neglect hearing was held in September, 1991, and Haynes-Seaman was Prowers County's star witness. On the witness stand, she not only alleged Carr had abused Pedro and four other students, but also named the students he had allegedly molested.

Carr's attorney cross-examined the unlicensed psychologist. She admitted she had never met or interviewed the four other students. The attorney then called Carr to the stand.

The teacher explained how Pedro had come to stay with him, and he denied Ms. Lopez's allegations of abuse.

Pedro was the last to testify. The boy, now in sixth-grade, answered in short, clipped sentences. Carr looked into the boy's eyes as he testified and felt hollowness in his stomach. The sadness that had been vanquished in their time together had returned, more prominent than ever. In his halting style, Pedro expressed his desire to stay with Carr.

The defense rested. Less than an hour later, the ruling was announced. The judge had discounted Haynes-Seaman's testimony and officially cleared Carr of wrongdoing. Despite the finding, the judge's hands regarding custody were tied. The judge determined Carr did not have a right to the child, and Pedro was returned to his mother.

As the boy left the courtroom, he looked at Carr and tried to smile. Then, reminiscent of the boy's earlier speech pattern, Pedro said only one word. "Goodbye."

The Termination Hearing

The court's verdict left Carr in a depressed mood. Despite his noble intentions, Carr was worried that the legal proceedings had damaged Pedro's fragile mental state. The thought that Pedro would have trouble forming a lasting bond with another adult weighed heavily on Carr's mind. Carr's only solace from his dark thoughts came from the realization that he would be able to return to the classroom. The reprieve from his guilt was short lived. Carr would never see the inside of a Bristol classroom again.

On August 16, 1991, the *Denver Post* ran a story on the third page of the local section headlined, "*Teacher to work despite custody, abuse case*." The story detailed the accusations of abuse against Carr and the result of the dependency and neglect hearing. The story quoted Carr as saying that he was looking forward to returning to the classroom. Because Carr was found innocent during the dependency and neglect hearing, he had been reinstated for the coming school year.

Following the story, the school board was inundated with letters from the community. Bristol residents were angry that a teacher, who was accused of sexually abusing a student, would be placed in contact with their children. In conjunction with the letters, community leaders started a petition to recall Carr from the Bristol City Council. Carr eventually lost his seat and was stripped of his position as the county chairman of the Republican party.

The school board heard the community's outrage and was forced to act. On August 31, 1991, two days before the school year was to begin, Bristol Public Schools Superintendent William Eddy again suspended Carr, with pay.

In a *Denver Post* article that ran the same day headlined, "*Dismissal of teacher sought; Bristol man at center of child-custody case*," Eddy told the reporter that he was sending a recommendation to the school board that Carr be terminated. Eddy did not elaborate on the reasons for termination. He stated only that "the recommendation to the board will be made for reasons I discussed with the teacher."

Following Carr's suspension, he contacted the CEA for representation.

"Carr had already been through a lot before I came on board," Lawler said. "The matter should have been resolved after the dependency and neglect hearing. I thought it was inappropriate to take disciplinary action after the legal system had exonerated him of all wrongdoing. I don't think I've ever seen a dependency and neglect hearing receive so much local press. I think the school board was being forced to take action because of the negative publicity."

Child Abuse Registry

Lawler had to overcome several obstacles before proceeding to the termination hearing. Because sexual abuse charges had been made, Carr's name had been placed on the Colorado Child Abuse Registry.

"Prowers County placed his name on the sex offender registry after he had been exonerated," Lawler said. "Besides humiliating my client, the County's actions had two results. First, the County was interfering in the custody case. No court would give a man on the sex offender registry custody of a child. The other was the more problematic issue for me. If Carr's name was on the sex offender registry, it would make any termination action easier to enforce and less prone to appeal. The County's move destroyed any chances my client had of resuming his political career or of returning to the classroom. From the timing, coming after he had been cleared of all wrongdoing, the move looked like a punitive measure by the county."

When asked to comment on the timing of the placement, Prowers County Director Fred Schmeir refused.

"It's obvious that the jury's verdict means nothing to these people," Carr said. "The jury found there was not a preponderance of evidence, but then some bureaucrat turns around and says there is a preponderance of evidence."

Lawler explained that a person who is found not guilty of all charges could be placed on the registry.

"The name of a person found not guilty can be placed on the registry if the County can show that a preponderance of evidence exists," Lawler said. "That was the loophole that Prowers County was using."

Lawler submitted a written request to have Carr's name removed from the list. He received a response two weeks later stating that because a backlog of cases existed, the request would not be heard for six months. The result of the delay was that Carr's name would remain on the registry during the coming termination hearing.

"That was really a tough blow," Lawler said. "Having his name on the list was grounds for termination. It looked like dirty pool on the County's part."

The day Lawler received the notice, he spoke to a *Denver Post* reporter. The next day, the *Denver Post* ran an article explaining the timing of Carr's name being placed on the registry. The story touched off an avalanche of complaints to Prowers County officials.

Less than two days after the story was published, Schmeir removed Carr's name from the sex offender registry.

"Carr's name was removed from the list the day before the *Denver Post* story ran," the *Denver Post* quoted Schmeir as saying.

Following Carr's removal, the Bristol Public Schools began an investigation. Superintendent Eddy was quoted in the *Bristol Daily News* as saying that new evidence had surfaced in the case.

"I wanted to know what the new evidence was," Lawler said. "When I asked him, he refused to tell me. I got more information from the newspapers than I did from district officials."

Eddy's new evidence was not presented until the school board began a termination hearing on December 23, 1991. Despite Lawler's assertions that there was no new evidence, the Superintendent claimed to the school board that he could prove, "Mr. Carr has circumvented and obstructed the role of the Prowers County Department of Social Services and has failed to comply with his legal responsibilities to report suspected child abuse."

"Eddy wasn't presenting hard evidence," Lawler said. "He'd

listened to KOA, a Denver radio station, interview Carr on August 17."

Tom Jensen conducted the interview. During the interview, Jensen asked Carr, "There has been abuse? Because she slapped him?"

"Yes," Carr answered.

"Did she slap him more than once?"

"From what he's told me in the past, yes," Carr replied. "And apparently, so [have] her boyfriends. I do believe there are other incidents of abuse and neglect."

Lawler believed the interview bolstered his client's case.

"Her decision to have a stranger raise her son was not born out of altruism toward her son," Lawler said. "She gave him up to help her own financial situation. Additionally, there were problems in her home. Everything Carr said in the KOA interview he testified to in the dependency and neglect hearing. There was no new evidence, and Eddy never submitted hard evidence to support his supposedly new charges."

Following the first day of the termination hearing, Eddy's written request for termination was printed in the *Bristol Daily News*. The written request restated the mother's allegations of abuse and claimed Carr had let Pedro watch R-rated movies while in his care.

Pedro never testified in the hearing. The board's decision was based on the record of the dependency and neglect hearing and Eddy's word against Carr's.

"The superintendent claimed that Carr should not be allowed to teach because the community's confidence in the school district would be shaken and that Carr might abuse another student," Lawler said.

The termination hearing concluded two days after it began. Under Colorado law, the board had twenty days to reach a decision. On January 10, 1992, the board voted 4-1 to terminate Carr. The school board issued a 35-page finding.

"It was tough to read 33 pages of a 35-page decision saying what a good man and teacher Carr is, then recommending his dismissal," Lawler said.

The board's decision was not based on the accusations of abuse against Carr or Eddy's new charges.

"The board ruled that Carr had violated the district's policy regulating the relationship between student and teacher," Lawler said. "By taking Pedro into his house and showing kindness, the board found that Carr had broken district guidelines. I think the real reason behind the decision was Eddy's argument that the school would receive a lot of negative publicity and parents would complain vigorously if Carr was allowed to teach in Bristol again."

Dan Minor cast the one dissenting vote. Prior to the vote, Minor had pleaded with Board members to allow Carr to teach again.

"The majority of the charges by Eddy for dismissal were proven false," Minor said during an open session. "I feel we should let him continue teaching and not dismiss him. Carr is an excellent teacher."

The Appeal and the Aftermath

Lawler worked with Sharon Dreyer to draft an appeal. The two attorneys immediately filed their motion with the Colorado Court of Appeals. He found it outrageous that Carr had been terminated for what he considered noble actions.

"He took care of a student," Lawler said. "If he had abused Pedro, that would have been different, but he was cleared of all wrong doing. My client should have been commended, not terminated."

The Colorado Appeals Court heard the case on May 14, 1992. Lawler presented legal arguments to the court. To be successful in the appeal, Lawler had to show that an error had been made during the termination hearing. Lawler asserted that the school district had improperly applied district guidelines to the fact patterns in Carr's case. Lawler further argued that no grounds for termination existed because the living arrangement had not affected Carr's ability to teach students.

The school district countered Lawler's arguments by asserting that the district guidelines had been followed in the termination hearing and that Carr's care of Pedro had violated the district guidelines. The school district claimed that when Carr took Pedro into his home, he lost the ability to be impartial and treat all students equally and created a distraction that hampered his students' ability to learn.

Lawler and Carr had to wait until April 15, 1993, for the court's ruling. The Colorado Court of Appeals found for the district. In their written opinion, the judges wrote that Carr had crossed the line between students and teachers and that he had created a situation detrimental to learning. The court further stated that sufficient grounds for termination existed.

The ruling ended Carr's teaching career in Bristol but did not preclude him from teaching again. Because he had been found innocent of all abuse allegations, Carr's teaching license had not been revoked. Despite his experiences in Bristol, Carr wanted to teach again. Carr believed that his legal troubles had made him a better teacher. Instead of discouraging him from taking an active role in his students' lives, Carr's belief that teachers need to address students needs had been cemented.

"Carr felt he couldn't teach the way he wanted to in Colorado," Lawler said. "Because of the media coverage, he would have found it difficult finding a job. He was cleared of all wrongdoing, but his name and reputation were tainted. He wanted to be fulfilled, so he knew he had to continue teaching."

Carr took a job teaching in Mexico where he is still teaching today. Despite his earlier dismissal, Carr sees to it that his students are fed, clothed and receive the medical attention they need.

"The area in which he is teaching is impoverished," Lawler said. "He says his days are long, and most of his money goes to his students, but he is happy. He still thinks about Pedro and worries about his well-being. He's helping kids in Mexico as a way to assuage some of his guilt about the outcome of his relationship with Pedro. He can't help the boy now, but he can help other kids in Pedro's position."

Chapter 10
Al Wilder

The Beginning

Al Wilder focused his attention on his students' faces. Through the spectacles on his hawkish nose, he saw that their attention was riveted to the video of Italian director Bernardo Bertolucci's epic classic, *1900*. The film depicts the rise of fascism in Italy from 1900 through World War II.

The tall and lanky teacher's senior Logic and Debate class was watching the 266-minute film for the second day. The curriculum of the course was designed to teach students to think critically, independently and intuitively. It was also designed to explain the different forms of political ideology, in historical context, to high school students and allow them to debate the pros and cons of each individual political party.

Wilder's curriculum was created for honors students. But that school year, the Columbine High School counseling department had enrolled many senior students in need of an elective credit into the course. As a result, the students in Wilder's class ranged in academic abilities from the class valedictorian to students that appeared to be borderline special education.

During March of the second semester of the 1995 school year, Wilder's students were studying socialism in its various forms. Wilder first chose to focus on one extreme form of socialism – fascism.

Fascism denies that the majority, by the simple fact that it is a majority, can direct human society. Fascism rejects the doctrine of pacifism; instead it views pacifism as an act of cowardice in the face of sacrifice. Fascists believe war alone brings up to its highest tension all human energy and puts the stamp of nobility upon people who have courage to meet it. To illustrate the human condition inherent with fascism, Wilder chose to show his class *1900*.

The story is told through the eyes of two boys, born on the same date, one rich and one poor. The boys, played by Robert De Niro and Gerard Depardieu, become lifelong friends despite their differences in economic and social class. The movie follows them through the course of their lives. The boys grow into adults and witness the rise, cruelty and eventual fall of fascism.

Wilder used the classic film to personalize the cruelty of fascism for his students. Within minutes, his own life would become a living lesson of modern day neo-fascism in America.

The Complaint

The lights in Wilder's classroom were turned off during the viewing of the film. As Wilder watched his students in the illumination of the television, the door to his classroom was thrust open and the lights in the room were turned on. As he squinted from the sudden change in light, Wilder saw two men walking briskly to the front of the classroom. Columbine Principal Ron Marshall and another teacher walked authoritatively to the front of the room.

The short and balding Marshall went directly to the television and turned it off. In a commanding voice that seemed akin to the fascist soldiers in Bertolucci's film, Marshall ordered Wilder to follow him to the office. Marshall also informed Wilder he was confiscating the video under school district guidelines which govern the viewing of controversial films. The teacher that had accompanied Marshall was to stay with the students while Wilder was absent.

Marshall led Wilder from the class to his office. Nothing was said between the two men as they walked. Marshall ushered Wilder into his office and closed the door behind him.

The principal informed Wilder that a parent had complained about the use of *1900* after the first day that the film was shown. As a result, Wilder was suspended, with pay, for showing a controversial film without parental permission slips.

"One of the students who should not have been in the class had complained to her parents and the parents had called the school,"

Wilder said. "Over my twenty-five year career I'd shown movies such as *Missing* and *The Killing Fields* without a complaint. I gave my students optional assignments or the ability to go to the library if the film made them uncomfortable. The girl hadn't listened enough to understand that she didn't have to watch the film.

"Principal Marshall had watched the film in his basement and was disturbed by a sadomasochistic scene in the second half of the film. I hadn't planned to show that portion to my students. Bertolucci used the scene to show that a corrupt politician is corrupt in his personal life. In context, the scene is important to the movie, but I knew it would make some students uncomfortable. I never got the chance to make the decision not to show that scene. The complaining girl just wasn't mature enough for the subject matter of my class."

Under Washington County School's District policy, the principal must be informed, in writing, of all planned teaching of controversial issues or use of controversial learning resources and explain their educational purpose. The written notice had to be given twenty days prior to showing the film. Wilder had not informed Marshall of his plans to present the movie to his students, and Marshall was adding a charge of insubordination as a reason for the suspension.

"The district policy on controversial materials also includes the duty of the principal to mediate a conversation between the offended parent and the teacher," Wilder said. "Principal Marshall had not and did not arrange that meeting. That violated district policy, and it wasn't the first time.

"A more prudent teacher would have gotten a permission slip for the individual movie, but I'd sent a blanket slip at the beginning of the year. The school district's policy didn't state a permission slip was necessary. I hadn't received any complaints about movies in the past. I didn't think there would be a problem this time, but Marshall was looking for a reason to get rid of me, and this was a golden opportunity for him."

After the conversation, Wilder left the school building and contacted the CEA of which he had been a member for years. Greg Lawler was in court at the time but called him back the next day.

"Al Wilder informed me of his situation," Lawler said. "A

reprimand seemed appropriate for the offense, and I didn't think it warranted a termination. When I shared my thoughts with Wilder, he explained the background of his relationship with Principal Marshall, and I realized that the situation was probably headed for a termination of Wilder's employment."

Past History

Wilder revealed to Lawler that he had a history of friction with Principal Marshall. He described a personnel record of sterling evaluations punctuated with six written reprimands for tardiness and neglect of duty. Wilder also asserted that Marshall was running Columbine High School like a neo-fascist.

According to Wilder, the reprimands in his file were for personal reasons in Wilder's life. They were all reasons known by Marshall.

"My responsibilities as a parent and my concern about my wife's health lead to absences and tardiness," Wilder said.

Complicating matters, Wilder was 61 at the time of his suspension and suffering from a prostate condition. Combined with caring for his ill wife, Wilder was late for school from time to time. Because of his tardiness, Wilder's colleagues were frequently asked to cover his classes.

The teachers at Columbine were sympathetic for a time but eventually grew to see Wilder's tardiness as an imposition. The school district alluded to the faculty's feelings in their Colorado Supreme Court filing. In the court document, the school district's attorneys wrote that, "The faculty eventually decided not to cover his class when they were being asked to nine times in a semester. This encroached on their obligations."

Despite knowing of Wilder's situation, Marshall gave the teacher several written reprimands when the faculty of the school complained to him.

Wilder was also late to class for professional reasons.

"Sometimes I'd be late for cafeteria duty," Wilder said. "Having been an assistant principal at a previous school, I knew the lunch room was always overstaffed with adults. I'd be on my way to cover my shift, and a student would stop me in the hall. I'd be late for my assignment because I was talking to a student."

When staff members complained, Marshall reprimanded Wilder. The two men were also at odds over their political beliefs.

The Harvard educated teacher's politics bent to the liberal side. Wilder sponsored a school group called the Zen Croquet Club. The club was school sponsored, and numerous honor students were members.

"We would meet in a park across from the school," Wilder said. "The club was comprised of student leaders. We would play croquet and just talk about philosophy. The name of the club was kind of a joke. I'd heard of Zen Golf, Zen Frisbee and so on. When I heard about those clubs in other schools, I came up with Zen Croquet."

Wilder's club became controversial when a non-sanctioned club of Christians wanted to become school sponsored. Principal Marshall denied the club's application to become an official school club based on the separation of church and state. The petitioning students were angry and used Wilder's Zen Croquet Club as the basis for their argument.

"They saw us in their yearbook and pointed out our page to Principal Marshall," Wilder said. "They argued that Zen was part of the Buddhist religion and that we were therefore a religious club. Principal Marshall then targeted the club for removal of school sponsorship."

The conflicts were not the last between Marshall and Wilder. Principal Marshall's political ideology was highly conservative, and he chaffed at Wilder's social views.

"For the most part, administrators use a benign form of fascism," Wilder said. "They have to be fascist to keep order enough to teach. Principal Marshall went to the extreme. I'd say he was a neo-fascist. He needed to control every aspect of the school in order to make himself look good. Principal Marshall had career aspirations. To advance his career, he needed to have his administration appear to be working, and he wasn't afraid to use ruthless tactics to accomplish that goal."

As an example, Wilder cites Marshall's actions during his tenure before Columbine.

"He censored the student newspaper at his previous school," Wilder said. "He stopped a potentially damaging story about a teacher from being published. Control of the media is a component of fascist states and he learned he could manipulate the media to his purpose prior to coming to Columbine."

At Columbine, Marshall continued his control over student media. Marshall oversaw a morning television show produced by students for a closed circuit broadcast. Marshall had the final say over what was broadcast, and he censored any material that reflected poorly on his administration.

"He ruled with an iron fist," Wilder said. "There were no means of contradicting his propaganda."

According to Wilder, another prong of Marshall's fascism was the school's athletics. Similar to the communist's use of sports to advance political ideology, Principal Marshall used Columbine's athletic teams to enhance the school's image and by correlation his career.

"Marshall created a win-at-all-costs environment," Wilder said. "Students that performed well athletically were treated deferentially. Students that weren't talented were heavily chastised and embarrassed by the coaches Marshall had hired. Those students then took their frustrations out on weaker students in their class, who then took their frustration out on lower classmen. This created a culture of bullying. That culture eventually led to the Columbine massacre. Even though a different principal was in charge by that time, he could not make enough changes to alter that bullying culture."

Throughout this time, Wilder was not outspoken during faculty meetings, but his social views marked him for dismissal with Principal Marshall.

"Principal Marshall, being a neo-fascist, wanted to surround himself with 'yes' men," Wilder said. "Because I didn't always agree with him, I was a political liability. He was looking for an excuse to 'Get Wilder' and he used this opportunity to his advantage."

Media Coverage Begins

After being briefed about the animosity between Wilder and Marshall, Lawler expected a recommendation for termination. His hands were tied until Principal Marshall acted officially.

The *Denver Post* broke the story of Wilder's suspension on August 9, 1995, with a headline that read "*Teacher in trouble over film.*" The story described Wilder's use of the movie *1900* and the school district's disciplinary options.

"The story came out while we were waiting for Principal Marshall to send his official recommendation to the school board," Lawler said. "At that time, Principal Marshall still had the option to recommend a written reprimand. The story accurately stated where we were in the process and that a termination hearing could not take place until Marshall recommended Wilder's dismissal. I'm not sure if the media coverage motivated Marshall to act swiftly, but he made his formal recommendation several days after the story broke. Often times, the press under reports the technical aspects of the termination process. I was surprised by the reporter's accuracy."

Following Marshall's official recommendation, Lawler applied for and was granted a termination hearing. The hearing was set to begin in November, 1995, but due to scheduling issues, the hearing was not held until February, 1996.

In the months leading up to the termination hearing, the media continued their intense coverage of the case. The news articles started an avalanche of letters to the editor. Soon, reports of the other teachers' frustration and Wilder's conduct, including the use of films, began to appear in the local newspapers.

"Some of Wilder's colleagues didn't like the fact he was using movies as an educational tool," Lawler said. "They thought that showing movies was lazy. Combined with Wilder's tardiness, the stories painted a picture of a deadbeat teacher.

"In reality, Wilder was a gifted teacher. Many students and teachers admired him for his innovative teaching techniques. Wilder augmented written assignments with movies to facilitate debates and encourage critical thinking skills."

As the media storm swirled around Wilder, Lawler began enlisting the aid of various anti-censorship groups. The National Coalition Against Censorship and the American Civil Liberties Union both supported Wilder.

Coalition members sent a letter in Wilder's defense to Colorado Governor Roy Romer. The letter was written and signed by film director Martin Scorsese. In the letter Scorsese wrote, "It is outrageous that Colorado school officials would attempt to fire a teacher for choosing to use a classic film as an instructional tool." Fellow Directors Milos Foreman and James Ivory, playwright Tony Kushner and author Judy Blume also signed the letter.

The ACLU assisted in Wilder's defense by obtaining the services of a prominent lawyer, Walter Gerash, whom Lawler had worked with in the past. Gerash took the case pro-bono.

"They were worried about Wilder's First Amendment rights," Lawler said. "They saw Marshall's recommendation for termination as an overt action of censorship. Gerash was famous locally for his successful defense of the United Bank Father's Day murder case. Along with another prominent co-counsel, Gerash had obtained an acquittal for the defendant, James King. Gerash was a tough courtroom litigator. We had a dream team for the termination hearing," Lawler said. "There are few termination hearings I can think of where a teacher was so well represented. Gerash was a great addition to Wilder's defense team."

The *Denver Rocky Mountain News* detailed Hollywood's defense of Wilder in a January 26, 1996, article headlined "*Teacher's plight draws spotlight*." After quoting Scorsese and the letter from the coalition, the article quoted Governor Roy Romer's spokesperson as saying that he "…did not wish to become involved."

Wilder's high-profile defense team was publicized by the media. In a February 6, 1996, article, the *Canyon Courier*, a local newspaper, ran an editorial criticizing Wilder's defense team. In the paper's opinion, titled "*Teacher's Union shows its colors*," the editor wrote that Wilder's defense team was trying to obfuscate the issues of the case.

The paper saw the issue as that of a negligent teacher facing dismissal for wrongful actions as opposed to the defense's assertion that Wilder's constitutional rights were being violated. The paper further alleged that the CEA was forcing its liberal views onto mainstream America.

"That was really an over simplification of our defense. There were many issues," Lawler said. "We weren't only arguing that the First Amendment rights of Wilder were at stake. We were arguing that the students were old enough to rent the film on their own. We were also arguing that the students had a right to see art and determine its value for themselves. These issues should have been important to a newspaper, but I believe the editors thought Gerash's presence in the case gave the trial an O.J. Simpson feel. It seemed to the newspapers like Wilder was trying to get off by stacking the legal deck."

The same day, a similar opinion ran in the *Denver Rocky Mountain News*. The paper's editors questioned whether movies were appropriate teaching tools. The editorial writers asserted that historical films often give fictional accounts for real events and are rarely accurate. Once again, Wilder's colleagues were quoted as saying that the teacher relied too heavily on films in his lesson plans, despite the fact that he'd only shown three films, including *1900*, over the course of the school year.

The next day, the *Denver Rocky Mountain News* ran a story about the impending termination hearing. The story detailed Wilder's history of tardiness and the written reprimands in his personnel file. After laying out the case against Wilder, the paper offered Lawler a chance to comment. Of the twenty column inches, Wilder's defense team was quoted in two sentences.

Lawler was quoted saying that, "The crime Wilder is guilty of is trying to present art." Lawler had actually given the quote to a reporter several weeks before. His short explanation of the quote was never reported.

"I described the film as a classic and told the reporter that the students were old enough to rent the movie," Lawler said. "That was all left out of the story. Despite the media's frequent use of First Amendment protections, it looked like they were aligning themselves with the school district. The newspaper gave the school district ample room to make its case but gave the defense only two sentences. Newspapers are supposed to be fair and balanced. You can argue whether or not their treatment of the defense was fair, but it definitely wasn't balanced."

Bertolucci's Involvement Begins

The National Coalition Against Censorship informed the Academy Award-winning director of *1900* of the events taking place in Colorado. Bertolucci was upset by what he heard. Prior to the termination hearing, the director called Wilder to offer his support.

Bertolucci was familiar with censorship from experiences in his own life. His 1973 film, *Last Tango In Paris*, was banned in Italy, and the Italian government criminally charged him.

"I was sentenced to two months of prison. The sentence was eventually suspended, though," Bertolucci said. "I could not vote for five years because of my conviction. Unfortunately, what went on in Colorado reminds me of that very, very horrible moment in my life."

Bertolucci pledged his support to Wilder and agreed to testify in the case if he was needed.

"My film is a historical epic about a period of history – of Italian history – which I don't think is very well known to young American students," Bertolucci said. "The idea of punishing Wilder was absolutely dark and medieval."

Bertolucci was outspoken in his defense of Wilder, and his comments were carried nationwide.

Lawler accepted Bertolucci's offer to testify. Before the termination hearing was concluded, the director had a chance to defend Wilder and his work.

The Termination Hearing

The day the termination hearing was to begin finally arrived. Outside the courthouse, cameras from every paper, television and radio station in town jammed the entryway of the building. As Lawler and Gerash ushered Wilder through the throng of reporters, Lawler spotted a *USA Today* cameraman.

"The case contained so many hot-button issues, such as First Amendment protections, that I wasn't surprised there was national media interest in the case. Also, the school district had done a good job with their public relations campaign. The case was bound to be picked up by the national press. News that Bertolucci planned to testify had also leaked out. It was already a high-profile case before that," Lawler said. "Bertolucci's presence made it more so."

The termination hearing lasted two weeks. Lawler presented Wilder's side of the story to the impartial hearing officer. Gerash, sitting second chair, gave advice to Lawler loudly enough to be heard by reporters in the room.

"Walter was older and didn't hear as well," Lawler explained. "He thought he was speaking softly, but everyone heard him. I laughed when I saw a report in the *Denver Rocky Mountain News* describing him as hissing at me. That was Walter's version of whispering."

Gerash grew to be a media favorite. Reporters flocked to him when he emerged daily from the courtroom. Gerash's daily quotes filled the headlines. After the first day of testimony, Gerash told reporters that the Wilder case was a witch-hunt. The next day, the *Denver Rocky Mountain News* ran a story with the headline, "*Attempt to fire teacher a witch hunt, Principal not employee is guilty Gerash charges.*"

Gerash was a seasoned veteran and knew how to play to the press.

"The school district had done a great job destroying my client's reputation through the various media outlets," Lawler said. "Walter was just trying to even our odds in the court of public opinion."

Lawler discovered that pushing through the daily herd of reporters who were vying for Gerash's attention was time consuming, but inside the courthouse, events were proceeding rapidly.

The school district's attorney, Alex Harpen, opened the proceedings and called the parents of the complaining girl to the stand. The parents testified their daughter was upset by the images of drug use and sex in the movie.

They claimed they had not given the girl permission to see the film, and they weren't aware that Wilder had provided his students with an option to go to the library. Under cross-examination by Gerash, the girl's parents acknowledged they had signed a permission slip covering all movies at the beginning of the year.

Harpen followed the parents' testimony with their daughter's. The girl testified she did not know that she didn't have to watch the film. Under cross-examination by Gerash, the girl admitted she had seen students go to the library during previous films.

Principal Marshall was the next to testify. Under Harpen's questioning, Marshall alleged that Wilder was negligent and derelict in his duties. The principal asserted that the previous warnings he'd given Wilder were enough to warrant termination and that Wilder's showing of *1900* was "…the straw that broke the camel's back."

Under cross-examination by Lawler, Principal Marshall agreed with the defense's assertion that Wilder had sent parents a blanket permission slip at the beginning of the year. Marshall also conceded the fact that he hadn't enforced the school district's controversial films policy for Wilder's past movies.

At the end of the first week of testimony, Lawler began arguments for the defense. Bertolucci was the first witness he called. Because the director was busy filming his next movie in Rome, his testimony was given via a conference call.

As Gerash questioned the director, Bertolucci's deep, rich voice boomed through the speakerphone.

"The puritanical urge to divorce the sexual material in my film from its context is only a prelude to a similar desire to cut politics and history from the context in which they are embedded," Bertolucci testified. "How will future generations grapple with the present if they cannot be allowed to bear witness to the past?"

Bertolucci was not cross-examined by Harpen. The director's testimony lasted less than thirty minutes.

"They couldn't impeach his testimony," Lawler said. "The film was and is a classic. There was no disputing that fact."

After Bertolucci's testimony, Lawler attacked the school district's argument that Wilder did not have a right to show the film. He pointed to the blanket permission slip and asserted Wilder had used a classic film as a teaching tool. Lawler also argued that Wilder had a First Amendment right to show the film.

The termination hearing then moved to closing arguments.

Harpen went first and criticized the defense's assertion that the blanket permission slip granted Wilder permission to show the film.

"Every member of the language arts department knew the policy," Harpen said. "If Mr. Wilder was ignorant of this policy, that in itself constitutes neglect of duty."

Gerash opened closing arguments for the defense.

"This case is about censorship," Gerash said. "This case is about thought control exercised by one individual who has violated due process and bypassed the basic precepts of our Constitution. There is a smell of fascism in the air."

Gerash then attacked the school district's policy on controversial films.

"The district's policy requiring prior approval of controversial material is unconstitutional because the definition of controversial is too broad and vague."

Lawler then took over arguments. To bolster his claim that Marshall's actions constituted censorship, Lawler showed the hearing officer a poster of Michelangelo's sculpture of a nude David.

"Marshall's view of *1900* would be like focusing only on David's groin," Lawler said. "Principal Marshall's version of art would be like putting a pair of boxer shorts on the classic work of art."

The hearing officer then took the matter under advisement. State law required a ruling within twenty days. Less than two weeks later, the hearing officer issued a decision. The finding was a mixed verdict for Wilder.

"The hearing officer found that my client's actions constituted a neglect of duty and insubordination," Lawler said. "The finding was based on his history of tardiness which was caused by traumatic issues in his personal life. The hearing officer took Wilder's personal life into account and recommended Wilder's reinstatement."

Even with the hearing officer's recommendation for reinstatement, Lawler knew that the school board could still vote to terminate Wilder's contract. For Wilder, the school board's vote for termination was a foregone conclusion.

"Jefferson County was a conservative district at the time," Wilder said. "The school board was comprised of three moderate conservatives and two hard-liners who were gaining influence. I knew a hearing before the school board would be biased against my case."

The School Board Hearing

On April 2, 1996, the Jefferson County School Board called an emergency meeting to discuss Wilder's teaching contract. Principal Marshall started the proceedings by showing the board a nineteen-minute video he had created using the school's media room.

The abridged version contained every scene of nudity, sex and violence in *1900*.

"Principal Marshall used a sadomasochistic scene in the second half of the movie, along with other scenes of nudity and drug use, to show that the film was controversial. Those scenes were necessary to show the moral corruption of the fascist character," Wilder said. "Taken out of context, the scenes looked gratuitous. What the director was demonstrating was that power corrupts professional and personal lives. At its core, *1900* is a morality play, full of symbolism. The fascist character wears a black trench coat. The movie's symbolism clearly delineates between good and evil."

Lawler argued that Wilder should not be dismissed because the district's policy about the use of controversial films was vague and unevenly enforced.

"The district policy did not even call for permission slips," Lawler explained. "Controversial films had been shown by other faculty members with no parental complaints or punitive measures by Marshall. The reason Principal Marshall was enforcing the guidelines in Wilder's case was personal."

Lawler also advanced Wilder's argument that a Logic and Debate class should promote critical thinking.

"During intense scenes, most teachers at Columbine would walk in front of the television screen to block the students' view of the images. Movies like *Romeo and Juliet* were routinely censored by teachers," Wilder said. "By censoring the sexual scenes in Shakespeare's play, the teachers were making the act of sex taboo. They were actually giving the images greater importance.

"Censoring movies also takes away the ability of students to think independently and make up their minds about the actions in the film for themselves, which was the point of the class."

The next day, Wilder's assumption about the school board's eventual ruling was proven correct. The Jefferson County School Board voted 5-0 for his dismissal. The *Denver Rocky Mountain News* reached Bertolucci in Rome following the decision, and the director expressed his "profound disquiet" over the ruling.

"School district officials were medieval when they tried to fire him," Bertolucci said. "The school board's actions were insulting to me personally. Punishing Wilder was nothing short of fascist censorship."

The decision gave Lawler and the ACLU a sense of unease as well. Through the facilitation of an ACLU spokesperson, the *New York Times* ran a story in the paper's Sunday edition. The story detailed Wilder's ordeal and suggested students could see R-rated films on their own. The paper further wrote that if the students were exposed to R-rated material on their own, why wasn't it permissible in schools?

On April 3, 1996, the *Rocky Mountain News* ran an editorial defending Wilder. The same paper that had been critical of Wilder from the beginning of its coverage was now arguing that Wilder's termination chilled academic freedom.

"The editorial stated that the paper wished us well with our appeal to the Colorado Court of Appeals. I think the media's attitude changed when they realized the paper's First Amendment rights would be damaged if my client was unsuccessful in court and a negative legal precedent was established," Lawler said.

The Colorado Court of Appeals

The CEA and the ACLU filed their appeal two months after the board's ruling. The issue went before the Colorado Court of Appeals in January, 1997.

Dreyer argued that Wilder had a constitutional right to show the film, that the district's policy regarding the viewing of controversial films was vague and that state law did not allow for termination.

Harpen, the school district's attorney, countered Lawler's arguments with Wilder's past history of tardiness and insubordination.

"The issues Harpen raised weren't relevant to the case," Lawler said. "The issue was my client's actions with regard to the showing of *1900*. Prior to oral arguments, the newspapers' editorial pages had been defending my client, and they knew that the school district's stance was growing unpopular. To win back the public, the school district had to change tactics and rely on Wilder's shortcomings."

The Colorado Court of Appeals overturned the school board's decision and ordered Wilder reinstated. The school district immediately appealed the decision to the Colorado Supreme Court.

"They couldn't let it go at that," Lawler said. "Because of the intense media scrutiny of the case, Jefferson County Schools would lose face if they didn't continue with the appeals process. The media was bound to report, in-depth, that the school had backed down. Dropping the case would have also created the potential of a civil suit on behalf of Wilder. They had to go the distance."

The Colorado Supreme Court

The Court of Appeal's ruling was stayed while the Colorado Supreme Court decided whether or not to grant the school district's motion. In November, 1997, the Colorado Supreme Court agreed to hear the case.

Oral arguments began less than two weeks later. Both sides advanced the same arguments that they had made in previous hearings. When oral arguments concluded, the wait for a ruling began.

"I was a little leery of the court's makeup," Lawler said. "At that time, the court was weighted with conservatives, similar to the make-up of the Jefferson County School Board. In previous years, the court had not been sympathetic to First Amendment issues in the classroom. Governor Romer was a liberal, but he'd not had many chances to appoint Colorado Supreme Court judges. I think conservative judges generally do not conceive of First Amendment rights with elasticity the way liberal judges are more apt to."

The Colorado Supreme Court ruled during the first week of January in 1998. With the exception of two judges who drafted a minority opinion, the court found that the First Amendment did not protect Wilder from termination, that Wilder had violated the school district's controversial film guidelines and that sufficient grounds for termination existed.

In the dissenting opinion, the writing judges stated, "Wilder…was an innovative teacher. When asked if he had objected to previous movies Mr. Wilder had shown, Principal Marshall said he had not. The content of *1900* was educational and informative. The scenes shown the school board were no worse than scenes contained in the movies Principal Marshall had not objected to."

The dissent also stated that Marshall's nineteen-minute version of the film was the only objectionable film in the case. The dissenters wrote that Wilder was protected by the First Amendment and no grounds for termination existed.

Wilder considered appealing to the United States Supreme Court but decided not to.

"The United States Supreme Court was also very conservative," Lawler said. "I didn't think we'd have any better luck there. Should Wilder have appealed to the Supreme Court and lost, it could have been a damaging blow to teachers across the nation."

Following the case, Marshall's tactics seemed to benefit his career. He was promoted to an area superintendent position with the Jefferson County Schools. He held the position for several years before he retired.

Wilder moved to Massachusetts where he currently resides. He is not teaching. Wilder's plight still bothers many former students and parents at Columbine High School. In a letter to the editor, a parent of a former student lamented Wilder's fate.

Mary Murphy wrote that her daughter was about to drop out of school when she enrolled in Wilder's course. With the lessons Wilder taught and his encouragement, the girl went on to the University of Northern Colorado where she received her teaching degree. Murphy wondered how many students could have made something of their lives if Wilder had been allowed to resume his teaching career.

Wilder still maintains that the friction between Principal Marshall and himself was the catalyst for his dismissal. He finds it ironic that during a lesson about fascism, he would personally experience what he considered to be the human toll of a fascist regime.

The Columbine Massacre

The events, psychology and social pressures that led to the Columbine massacre are many and varied. Lessons learned in the Wilder case take on greater importance in the aftermath of the school's tragedy.

Just over a year after the Colorado Supreme Court ruling,

Dylan Klebold and Eric Harris stormed into Columbine High School with guns blazing. Harris and Klebold had considered themselves outsiders. The teens symbolized their friendship by wearing black trench coats similar to those worn by the fascists in Bertolucci's film.

While the boys' torment is only one aspect of the killers' psychology, the Wilder case gives a startling insight into an aspect of school life prevalent in schools across the nation. In America's push for higher educational standards, society has inadvertently created the need for what Wilder considers fascist regimes within the educational system. The result of this benign fascism is an increased competition among students.

That competition fosters a student caste system that creates a friction between students and between the faculty and administration. Faculty members are evaluated based on standardized test scores. Teachers who use innovative techniques that don't immediately reflect on standardized test scores are more likely to receive lesser evaluations than their peers who teach for the tests. The curtailment of new methods of teaching by administrators often leads to a natural mistrust between the faculty and administration and between conformist and non-conformist teachers.

The Colorado Legislature held an inquiry into the Columbine Massacre and uncovered some of the reasons that the boys' warning signs went undetected. The inquiry found that friction between the administration and faculty, along with friction between faculty members, had broken down the lines of communication in the school.

That same lack of communication was evident in the Wilder case. Marshall had numerous opportunities to facilitate a discussion between the teacher and the offended parents. The principal also had numerous opportunities to correct Wilder's use of controversial films, and he had a chance to offer Wilder a written reprimand and training for his non-compliance with district guidelines. Marshall failed to communicate with Wilder, and his treatment of the teacher led to the destruction of Wilder's career.

Members of American society are currently debating how to best deal with accusations of abuse against teachers. The national trend is to limit the legal protections afforded teachers. By stripping teachers of their protections against prosecutions arising from actions taken in the daily course of their duties, teachers' efforts to limit some students' escalating destructive behavior have been adversely affected. Teachers who discipline students are now subjected to retaliatory accusations of abuse.

The Wilder case is a microcosm of the friction between teachers, administrators and students in every school across the nation. The actions of Klebold and Harris should be examined for their commonality with all schools. The sociological variables that drove two young men to massacre fellow students were bullying and a lack of communication. The variables should be addressed through legislation and education for students, parents and educators to prevent further school shootings – but only after the root of the problem is examined and diagnosed. The Wilder case highlights the symptoms of the illness. It is up to society to proactively search for the cure.

Guilty Until Proven Innocent

Chapter 11

Robert Colin

The Beginning

Robert Colin was a highly respected Colorado sixth grade teacher in the Lincoln County School District, where he had taught for 24 years. Nominated three times for Teacher of the Year in his district, Colin had won the award twice. He also was a finalist for Teacher of the Year in Colorado in 1996.

With his deep, authoritative voice and prematurely gray hair, Colin's style and presentation in the classroom seemed better suited to a college than the middle school in which he taught. School administrators, who placed him in the role of mentoring young teachers, admired his teaching techniques.

In 1996, Colin applied for and was appointed to an exchange position in England and he spent the year teaching abroad in Manchester. By all accounts, Colin was the perfect ambassador for the American educational system. He returned to Colorado in 1997, invigorated by his travels.

Colin's overseas experiences exposed him to new methods and styles of teaching, and he was excited to share his insights with his colleagues. In 1998, despite his intentions, Colin's experiences with the criminal justice system would be the most valuable lesson he could impart to colleagues.

The events that changed his career started innocently. Colin was lecturing to his class about the Revolutionary War. As a history teacher, he'd given the same speech for twenty-four years. Colin's experiences had taught him to keep his students involved and to make the discussion relevant to their lives. To do that, he needed to encourage student participation.

Colin facilitated a class debate regarding the two other men who rode with Paul Revere during his famous ride and whether or not they deserved equal credit in the history texts.

His students were enjoying the discussion, except for two girls in the back of the room. As their classmates debated, the two girls whispered and giggled with each other. Colin had witnessed this same scene numerous times and the girls' grades were beginning to reflect their lack of participation.

Missy Carter, a petite, blonde-haired, blue-eyed girl, was usually the instigator of the chatter. She was popular with her peers and was the leader of her small clique.

Jessie Hamilton, Carter's friend, had large, brown eyes and long, black hair. Hamilton had developed physically earlier than most girls her age, and her self-esteem was low from the constant teasing she took from jealous girls. The girl was intelligent but, because of her self-worth issues, was a follower. Colin thought Hamilton would benefit by not sitting next to Carter, so he separated them.

The girls were angry about their new seating arrangement, and argued exhaustively with Colin. When the school bell rang, the girls stormed from the class and ran for their bus. Colin assumed their anger would pass quickly, but he was wrong.

That night, Missy went to her mother in tears and told her she didn't want to go back to Mr. Colin's class. Mrs. Carter pressed Missy for details and Missy told her that Colin had hugged her and moved his hands to her breast.

"I wasn't sure what Missy wanted me to do," Mrs. Carter testified in a hearing. "I didn't want to make trouble at school. I thought it might have been an accident. Mr. Colin was so respected; I couldn't believe he'd do anything like that. When Missy told me it wasn't the first time that something like that had happened, I knew I had to say something. I wasn't sure if he'd molested her, but I didn't want him touching my daughter."

Missy wanted her mother to write a note to Colin telling him to stop touching her, but Mrs. Carter thought more needed to be done. The next day Mrs. Carter went to Principal Lisa Phillips' office to report the incident. Phillips was stunned by the accusation, and she called Missy to her office. Missy repeated the same story to the principal that she'd told her mother. Phillips took the accusation seriously, but needed evidence to corroborate Missy's story before considering disciplinary action against Colin. Missy told Phillips that her friend, Jessie Hamilton, had witnessed the incident.

Phillips called Jessie to her office. Hamilton told the exact same story, verbatim, that Carter had. Hamilton went further with her story, claiming Colin had touched her on numerous occasions. Hamilton claimed Colin had tickled her when she raised her hand in class, but "had gone too far" and tickled her breast.

Phillips notified the sheriff's department and placed Colin on suspension, pending the outcome of the investigation.

After his suspension, Colin called the Colorado Education Association. Greg Lawler took the case. Lawler cautioned Colin that there was not much that could be done until the District Attorney took action or the school board terminated him. Lawler hired a private investigator to begin looking into the allegations and waited for the school district to make the next move.

"Until action is taken, teachers are in a wait-and-see mode. With Colin's solid reputation, I didn't think any charges would be filed," Lawler said. "I also expected the school would back him up, since there were no grounds for termination. I was wrong on both counts."

The Washington County Sheriff's office contacted the District Attorney's office. Laura Dunst, an assistant District Attorney, was assigned to oversee the investigation. Dunst was an attorney with a reputation as a fierce litigator. She specialized in sexual assault cases and saw justice for the victims as her personal responsibility. Her conviction rate was high, but her peers questioned the overzealous nature of some of her prosecutions.

Dunst immediately requested that the county psychologist, Roger Lewis, interview the alleged victims. Because of Colin's credentials, Dunst didn't want her case to come down to the students' words against Colin.

Dunst wanted Lewis to testify that Colin fit the profile of a molester. Dunst also instructed the sheriff's department to canvass the school for other victims. Before the investigation was over, seven students, five girls and two boys, made allegations of inappropriate touching by Colin. The other six accusing students all rode the bus to school with Missy except for one of Colin's former students. All students, save Colin's former student, told the same story. Colin's former student reported his allegation of abuse following the intense media coverage, but his claims were so unbelievable as to be incredible.

"The boy's allegations were his response to the media coverage," Lawler said. "His allegations are an illustration of how the media impacts teacher abuse cases."

Public Support and Outrage

While the sheriff's investigation continued, the community began asking questions. Parents of Colin's past and present students, as well as other teachers in his middle school, began pressuring the school to reinstate Colin. They believed a good man was being railroaded.

The parents held a meeting to discuss their dealings with Colin and tried to find a way to help him. The meeting was held late in October, 1998, in the home of one of Colin's students. Colin's colleagues were also present to show their support. Dunst, although uninvited, represented the District Attorney's office at the meeting.

During the meeting, the parents and teachers shared stories about what a moral and kind man Colin was. Among the glowing testimonials were accounts of Colin staying after school with students to provide them social guidance and further instruction on lessons the students did not fully grasp. Colin provided parents with a means of interacting in the educational process by calling them regularly and apprising them of their child's strengths and weaknesses. He gave them advice on how to improve the student's academic success.

Several teachers from the school attested to Colin's mentoring of young teachers. They cited him as a role model. They stated that by following Colin's example, they were better able to connect with their own students.

Dunst listened, seeming uninterested, throughout the meeting. She jotted notes as the parents spoke and made sounds of annoyance when anyone characterized Colin as a good man. She was especially disdainful of the teachers who testified Colin was a positive example to them.

As the meeting began to lose energy and long periods of silence filled the room, Dunst asked the group for a chance to speak. She began by reassuring the parents she wasn't trying to destroy a good man, but she was trying to protect the students.

"Colin may appear to be a good teacher, but he fits the profile of a molester developed by our psychologist, Roger Lewis," she said. Dunst listed the different criteria for the profile. A trusted teacher was her first example. A man that students go to with problems is a likely molester because he builds a trusting relationship with both the victim and their family. A child is less likely to tell a parent about inappropriate touching or behavior out of a fear that the parents won't believe them. Dunst asked them if they believed the accusing students' stories.

"The fact you're all here tells me you don't," Dunst pointed out. Dunst listed the next prong of the profile as a teacher that is loved by the community because the sex offender uses his reputation as a shield from allegations. She asked the group if anyone could refute the fact that Colin was such a man.

"The fact Colin is such a respected teacher is the reason you should trust him the least," Dunst told the group.

She cautioned the gathering that they were hindering her investigation and hurting their own children in the process.

"We have too many victims for the allegations to be fabricated," she said. "If it was one girl making these claims, you might be right. But the number of victims shows a clear pattern on the part of Mr. Colin. Any child in Colin's class is in severe jeopardy. I don't want any more victims. Do you?"

Lawler heard about Dunst's statements at the meeting and was incensed. "With that profile, every good teacher in the state should be in prison. The fact his exemplary record was being used to show Colin was a molester was incredibly unfair. It made me question the objectivity of the investigation."

The parents left the meeting stunned and bewildered. How had they not seen Colin was such a monster?

Media Maneuvers

The October meeting was a turning point in the public's perception of the case. Prior to the meeting, the school board had received numerous letters in Colin's defense. After the meeting, the board received no positive communication from the public.

"The prosecution knew its case was unpopular," Lawler explained. "The fact Dunst was present at the meeting tells me she was aware of that. Her comments at the meeting were the first salvo in her public relations campaign against my client. This was the type of underhanded tactic we had to deal with throughout the case."

On November 6th, the *Denver Post* ran its first story about the allegations. The story cited unnamed sources in law enforcement that Colin had allegedly molested seven students and charges were pending. The story contained numerous factual errors.

A week after the first story appeared, Lawler received a phone call from the Washington County District Attorney. They were officially filing charges against Colin and needed to make arrangements for his surrender.

"I told them we would cooperate in any way necessary. I wanted them to interview my client because the sheriff's office hadn't done that during their investigation. Colin had not been allowed the opportunity to tell Principal Phillips his side of the story, let alone the District Attorney," Lawler said. "Before a life and career were ruined, at a minimum it was reasonable he get to tell his side of the story with his attorney present to avoid having his words twisted into ammunition for the prosecution."

Lawler contacted his client and told Colin that he would arrange for Colin to give a statement at the Washington County Sheriff's office on the afternoon of November 13. Colin was anxious to tell his side of the story, but he wanted a chance to put his family and business affairs in order. The District Attorney's office agreed with the timeline. Lawler assured Colin that no arrest would be made until he had a chance to give his statement, per Lawler's conversation with the police and District Attorney's office.

After he hung up, Lawler called his investigator for a status report. The private investigator informed Lawler he was still interviewing students, but his progress was slow. The students' parents were reluctant to let their children speak with anyone related to Colin's defense team. Lawler encouraged him to be as expedient as possible.

After arranging his statement, Colin went for a walk in his neighborhood. Colin wanted to clear his mind and focus on what it would take to fight the charges. As he walked with his golden retriever down the street, Colin noticed a helicopter flying overhead. He could barely read the News 4 logo, the local NBC affiliate, on the side of it.

Assuming it was probably a traffic copter, he kept walking. Halfway up his block, Colin was suddenly surrounded by squad cars.

Officers stepped out of the cars, pointing their guns at him. They were yelling loudly and gesturing to the ground. It took a moment for Colin to understand what was happening. He slowly moved to his knees and then lay face down on the hot pavement. The officers rushed to Colin. He felt a knee press sharply into the small of his back. Colin put his hands behind his back and felt the cold steel of handcuffs snap around his wrists.

An officer lifted Colin to his feet and turned him so he faced a crowd of photographers. Multiple flashes partially blinded him. Colin tried to duck his head to hide his face, but more flashes filled his eyes. The picture on the front page of the *Denver Post* the following day pictured Colin with his head down, as if in shame.

Colin was placed roughly into the back of one of the squad cars. Before the officer slammed the door closed, Colin noticed several neighbors staring out the window at him. Despite his innocence, a wave of embarrassment washed over him. Colin knew he could never fully regain his reputation in the community.

"I was really outraged," Lawler said. "The action was unnecessary because we had made it clear that Colin was not a flight risk. He wanted to clear his name. The police later apologized to me. They stated they couldn't tell me who made the order to arrest, but they said it with a knowing wink because we all knew who was responsible. I can't prove she called the media to tip them about the arrest, but it fits with the way she handled the rest of the case. Colin's humiliation was just a game to her. She was trying to beat him down, to make him want to take a plea."

Colin was taken to county jail and fingerprinted. The teacher was then advised of the charges against him. Colin was charged with twenty-one counts of sexual assault by a person in a position of trust.

After posting ten thousand dollars bond, Colin was released that evening. He went home to be with his wife. That evening, the couple watched television. Colin was hoping for a few hours of escape from the horror that had suddenly filled his life. Escape was impossible. During the commercial breaks between shows, Channel 4 promoted their nightly newscast with scenes of his arrest.

Out of morbid curiosity, Colin watched the news story about him. Friends and neighbors were interviewed for the stories. He was saddened to see no one come to his defense.

"This was an innocent teacher, but because of the publicity, parents in the district didn't want their children in his class. Parents threatened to open enroll and go to a different district if Colin was allowed to teach again," Lawler said. "Because I had just begun my investigation, there was no way to counter the stories in the media. Every time a reporter asked me a question, I could only answer 'No comment.' In the media, a 'No comment' looks like an admission of guilt."

Lawler's Investigation

Lawler's investigator was making progress. He'd been granted permission to interview students, in addition to the accusers, that rode the bus with Missy Carter. The investigator told Lawler he'd uncovered the origin of Colin's problems.

"We discovered that the afternoon the girls were separated, they'd been complaining to the other kids on the bus. Soon, the conversation turned from how mean Mr. Colin was to what a pervert he was," Lawler said. "The story quickly grew to 'He touched my breasts.'"

Lawler's investigator also spoke to students in Missy Carter's other classes. They claimed Carter and Hamilton, as well as the other alleged victims, were bragging about how they got Mr. Colin in trouble and possibly fired.

Lawler was encouraged by the findings. As part of pretrial discovery, he provided written affidavits of the statements to Dunst. She ignored them. Dunst's evidentiary motions indicated to Lawler that the prosecutor had every intention of proceeding to trial.

The Resolution

Prior to the discovery hearing for the case, Lawler brought in his mentor, Craig Truman to help with the case.

"There were hours of interviews to go through," Lawler said. "Missy Carter's session was the first transcript we reviewed, and her statements looked damaging. Her version of events appeared to be a textbook example of a victim of molestation. Once we began looking at the other students' transcripts, we discovered that the prosecution had severe problems."

The six students that supported Missy Carter's claims with allegations of their own were subjected to hours of interviews with Lewis. Washington County has a program for victims of abuse that trains them how to testify at trial. The prosecutor was using the program and the therapy to not only gather evidence, but also to prep her witnesses for the trial, a common practice when dealing with underage witnesses.

The children's stories were consistent at first. The students described their feelings about the alleged abuse the exact same way Missy Carter had earlier. As the hours progressed, however, the psychologist's records revealed that the students began to change their stories. With the exception of Missy, all of the students claimed that the assaults had never happened. The transcripts quoted the children as saying that they were pressured by Missy to lie and told what to say.

Jessie Hamilton, Missy's friend, informed Lewis that Missy had been a victim of sexual assault in the past and knew exactly what to say to be believed. Over a period of weeks, Missy had coached the group during their bus rides to school.

The cool clique that Missy Carter led was currently shunning the students that had refused to go along with Missy's story. Because of the adolescent need to fit in, the accusing children had gone along with her plan.

"At that point in the interview, Lewis threatened the children," Lawler said. "The record clearly reads that Lewis told the children the case was too far along and that they'd get in trouble if they changed their statements. The students were telling the truth earlier but were lying when they recanted their testimony, Lewis claimed. The psychologist told the kids it was natural for victims of molestation to deny they were sexually assaulted. The fact the students recanted their testimony was actually an indication they were telling the truth earlier. Over the next two hours, the students gradually began telling their original stories."

Lawler and Truman were dumbfounded by the records of the sessions with Lewis. Truman told Lawler the case should not have proceeded as far as it had, and he wanted to keep the case from going to trial. Truman reasoned that Colin needed to be spared further humiliation. He also worried about the long-term psychological damage that would be inflicted on the children if they were forced to lie in court.

Truman was a well-known attorney in the state with many contacts. One of them was Mark Welsch, the Washington County District Attorney. The two men weren't friends, but they respected each other professionally.

Truman hoped Welsch, Dunst's boss, would listen and stop the case before it progressed further. Truman requested a meeting the week before the case was set for trial. Welsch granted Truman's unusual request. The meeting was scheduled just two days before opening arguments were to begin.

Lawler and Truman presented their case to Welsch and he listened attentively. Lawler began by explaining Missy Carter's past history of sexual abuse. She knew what she needed to say to be believed. Lawler explained the impetus for the charges – two friends being separated.

Next, he handed the District Attorney the record of his investigation, including the interviews of the students on Missy's bus. The statements clearly demonstrated the progression of the discussion to an allegation of sexual assault. By all accounts, Missy Carter was the instigator of the discussion.

Lawler presented his bombshell to Welsch. Lawler presented

a highlighted copy of the psychologist's criminal profile and his interview records. Lawler provided evidence that the students recanted their original statements and were forced back into their original stories by Lewis.

Welsch was appalled. He told Lawler and Truman that there wasn't evidence to warrant a trial. He further stated that a proper investigation should have cleared Colin. The District Attorney believed the evidence of innocence had been there all along, but it had been used improperly by Dunst to show guilt.

Welsch immediately dropped all charges against Colin. Dunst, however, was not formally reprimanded by the District Attorney's office for her conduct, and she remains in her position as a prosecutor of sexually based crimes.

The students who made false allegations were not disciplined. State law makes provisions for such instances in the form of false allegation charges. The school district also failed to punish the students involved despite the school district policy dictating that the students should have been suspended.

"There needs to be a law mandating disciplinary action against students who destroy teachers' lives with false allegations," Lawler said. "As the situation stands now, the decision to punish is left to the school district and prosecutor's office. Both are adversarial to the victim of the false allegation. There should be no choice in the matter. There needs to be zero tolerance for false allegations. Mandatory repercussions for false allegations will save careers."

Lawler saw the pretrial dismissal of all charges against his client as a full exoneration. Colin was excited by the news, and he thought his nightmare was over. With his name cleared, Colin expected to return to his position immediately. Colin's expectations went unfulfilled.

"He had every reason to expect the school district to welcome him back with open arms," Lawler said. "He had been their golden boy. There wasn't a teacher in the district with more accolades than Colin. The school district should have apologized to my client and moved on. But, the way the district treated Colin is a defining example of a teacher's inability to fully clear his name, even after the legal system finds him innocent. The general belief of the public is that the charges were brought for a reason. He may have been innocent, but Colin had to have done something wrong to warrant an arrest."

Colin was kept on suspension while the district figured out what to do with him. Angry parents were calling the school, threatening to pull their students from Colin's class. Letters to the editor from concerned parents were published in the local paper complaining that the school was not doing enough to protect their children. They were agitated that the school was thinking about putting a child molester back in the classroom.

Because of the intense media scrutiny and public outrage the case received, the school district believed it could not allow Colin back into the classroom. The negative publicity they would receive should the district have reinstated Colin would be overwhelming. School district officials were also worried about a possible civil suit by Colin.

To pre-empt the civil action, the district offered Colin a golden retirement package. One of the conditions of the package was a waiver of any civil liability. Colin was unwilling to go through a lengthy civil suit where he would have to relive the events that had destroyed his career. Colin accepted the retirement package.

Colin thought his reputation had been shattered nationwide. Whether real or imagined, every time he saw one of his neighbors, Colin saw suspicion in their eyes. Tired and ashamed, Colin moved to California.

Embittered by his experiences, he decided not to seek employment as a teacher. Instead, Colin found work in another field. He started a second career, at age 53, in construction. By pounding nails for a living, Colin hopes to pound out the frustration caused by his legal experience.

Chapter 12
Lori Salmon

The Beginning

Nick Van Exel head-faked a move to the left, cut hard right and slashed to the basket for an uncontested lay-up. In typical Denver Nuggets' style, he missed the open shot. Lori Salmon's students groaned.

Salmon caught the eye of the food vendor and motioned him over. The Nuggets' promotion she had taken her students to included free pizza. Salmon made sure each of the twelve children got a slice and settled in to watch the game. Normally, she took the best students in her class to games as a reward, but this game was different. Salmon had selected her class's poorest academic performers, hoping the night out would help motivate them to work harder so they could attend future games.

Salmon was a fifth-grade teacher at Gunnison County Elementary School in Fort Lupton, Colorado. The students in the district came from lower-class families, and Salmon knew that her students' parents could not afford to take their children to games. Over her twelve years at the school, her monthly trips to the Nuggets' games had become a regular event.

The game was a blow out. Salmon quickly lost interest in the game and began watching her students. She was particularly interested in Michael Burn. In class, Michael was inattentive and unresponsive. His row in her grade book resembled the score sheet of a baseball game – a lot of zeros.

As she watched him now, he was talkative and attentive. Michael educated his friends on the various nuances of the game. He explained the terms, plays and fouls to everyone around him who would listen. By just listening to him talk, Salmon realized that the boy was intelligent. That's why his academic performance troubled her so much. If the boy didn't begin doing his homework, she would have to hold him back a year. There was one option left to help the boy improve, but in order to implement her plan, she would need her principal's permission.

In the past, Salmon and other teachers had requested and been granted permission to use the vestibule in the small room adjacent to her classroom. Only students who were so far behind that they could never catch up on their own were sent to the room. Salmon placed those students in the room to complete late or missed assignments.

Often, the students would be in the room for an entire day, including their lunch period. Salmon would bring the students their lunch and collect their completed homework.

In the past, her method had been successful. She'd never had to hold a student back.

When the first period began, Salmon went to Burn, tapped him on the shoulder and asked the boy to follow her. Michael complied, and she led him to the small room. Salmon seated the boy in the vestibule and set a high stack of papers in front of Burn.

"If you don't get caught up, you are going to fail," Salmon said. "I'm giving you a chance to get caught up. I'm going to leave you in here every day until you complete these assignments. You'll miss class time, but you'll have enough work completed to pass. How does that sound?"

Michael shrugged his shoulders nonchalantly and grabbed the first assignment.

"I'll check on you to see if you need anything," Salmon said. "To make sure you can get all this work done, I'm going to have you work through lunch. I'll bring you food from the cafeteria or you can bring your own lunch. All right?"

Michael simply shrugged again. Salmon went back to her class and resumed her normal teaching duties. At lunch, she checked on Michael. The boy was working hard. Salmon gave him his lunch and picked up his finished work.

When she graded the work that evening, she noticed that Michael was making progress. His work was at a B-plus level.

Seeing the boy's progress, Salmon was satisfied her method was working.

For the next five days Salmon repeated the process. Michael never complained; he just worked through the mound of late assignments. Everything was fine until the sixth day. On January 14, 2000, Colorado's weather turned nasty. The wind howled, and snow began to blow across the unprotected plains town.

When Salmon placed Michael in the small room, she noticed that the room was chilly. Salmon knew an unheated room in a snowstorm could be uncomfortable, but Michael was dressed for the weather. He needed to endure the cold for only a few more days. Salmon made sure that Michael was wearing his winter coat and took him a blanket. Over the course of the day, she checked on him regularly and took the boy hot chocolate. Every time Salmon entered the small room, Michael complained that he was cold. When the day was over, Salmon could see that Michael's level of productivity had declined.

Despite the boy's slowing progress, Salmon decided to let him keep working. At his current pace, Michael would have enough assignments completed to pass her class within a few days. Salmon assumed Michael would be caught up within four days, but it actually took seven days.

When Michael was finished with all of his work, Salmon called his parents to let them know that their child was caught up on his assignments. Michael's parents did not speak much English, and Salmon did not speak much Spanish, but she figured that Mr. and Mrs. Burn needed to be involved in the process. When they thanked her, she hung up the phone and assumed they had understood.

Salmon had no way of knowing that not only did the parents not know what she had told them, but they had also been getting a completely different story from Michael. Unbeknownst to Salmon, Michael had been going home to his parents and telling them that Salmon was locking him in an unheated room for the entire school day. Michael never told his parents why he was in the room.

The Complaint

On Wednesday, February 1, 2000, Salmon was summoned to Principal Pañera's office. Pañera informed Salmon that Mr. and Mrs. Burn had complained to the school and that they were considering a civil suit against the school district and her personally.

Salmon was stunned. She asked to meet with the boy's parents to explain her actions, but Pañera denied her request. The principal explained to Salmon that it was in her best interest to remain quiet since Mr. and Mrs. Burn were considering a lawsuit.

Salmon thanked Pañera for the advice and started to leave the office, but Principal Pañera stopped her before she reached the door. Pañera explained to Salmon that he had to follow district guidelines regarding complaints. He was placing Salmon on suspension, with pay, pending the outcome of the police investigation.

"My actions were never questioned by you in the past," Salmon said. "How can you suspend me for actions you condoned?"

"Because that is the district policy, and I have to follow it," Pañera explained. "The school district is looking at a possible lawsuit, and I need to protect the district. I'm notifying the authorities and recommending your dismissal to the school board."

Salmon's shock was wearing off, and the feeling was replaced by unmitigated anger.

"Then you'll be facing a lawsuit from me as well," Salmon said as she left the office.

Salmon went home and called the Colorado Education Association. After several phone calls, she was put in touch with Greg Lawler.

The Investigation

Lawler contracted with an investigator to get written statements from Michael's parents and other students and teachers at Salmon's school. Lawler's investigator found evidence that bolstered Salmon's case.

"Salmon wasn't the only teacher using the vestibule to get students caught up," Lawler explained. "My investigator discovered that other teachers regularly put their students in the small room. It was clear that using the vestibule was condoned by the school district. Salmon was facing termination not for her actions, but for the way the media reported those actions initially. The district was trying to assuage the public's concerns and stave off any civil liability. If they admitted that what Salmon had done was supported by school officials, they opened the door for any parent of a child that had been placed in the vestibule to sue."

Because of the school district's perceived civil liability, Lawler anticipated the termination of Salmon's contract. Although the district could terminate her contract, Lawler did not believe the termination would hold up in court.

"The case was very simple," Lawler said. "The district knew what Salmon was doing and supported her; I didn't see a reason to dismiss her. If they did dismiss her, I believed that I had sufficient grounds to get her reinstated."

The Gunnison County Sheriff's Office was called in to investigate the charges. After interviewing Michael and his parents, the other students in Salmon's class, Principal Pañera and Salmon, the sheriff's office refused to file charges.

"They investigated and found that my client had done nothing criminal," Lawler said. "I think that would have been the end of it, but the local newspaper wouldn't let it go at that."

The Media Coverage

Lawler's belief that Salmon's case was simple was correct from a legal viewpoint, but he did not factor in the variable of public pressure. When the media began to cover Salmon's ordeal, the coverage changed the entire dynamic of the case.

"I originally thought that it would be a simple case, but it became a circus once the media covered it," Lawler said.

On April 8, 2000, the *Fort Lupton Tribune* ran the first story on the case. In the article headlined, *"Teacher cleared of charges, might face dismissal,"* the room Michael was placed in was described as a locked closet with no heat. The article quoted Mr. and Mrs. Burn as saying, "She [Salmon] made a grave mistake. If she's such a good teacher, I believe she needs to control the people in her classroom better."

The news account of the story ignited a firestorm of community outrage against Salmon. Letters to the editor questioning Salmon's actions ran every day. The school was flooded with calls from angry members of the community, demanding Salmon's termination.

"The media storm intensified after that," Lawler said. "At that point, only the parents' side of the story was being told. I needed to get Salmon's version of events into the public dialogue. To do that, I issued a press release."

Lawler's press release was sent to various media outlets and was reported by the local media. In a *Fort Lupton Tribune* article headlined "*Teacher may be dismissed from District 6*," Lawler's release was quoted as saying, "The indication is that the district is going to bring dismissal charges to the board. I think that's the direction they will go." Lawler's explanation of Salmon's actions was quoted extensively, while Superintendent Tony Como was left with a 'no comment.'

"Superintendent Como was still drafting his letter to the school board," Lawler said. "That's one of the few times I beat the school district to the punch. The media story put the school district on the defensive. That was a nice change for me. In all of my previous cases, I'd been left with a 'no comment.' Because of the implied guilt associated with a 'no comment,' catching the district off guard left me with a tactical advantage that would be crucial if the case ever found it's way to a court room."

The impact of Lawler's press release negated the damage done to the public's perception of the case from the first news accounts. The *Fort Lupton Tribune* article galvanized Salmon's supporters in the community who had been afraid to speak out until then.

The day after the news story, Salmon's supporters picketed outside the district 6 Educational Services building. Salmon's supporters waved signs that read "Honk for Lori." Numerous drivers passing by the protesters laid on their horns.

Superintendent Como still had not filed his official recommendation by the school board meeting on April 27. Despite the fact that Salmon's case was not on the agenda, Salmon's supporters packed the meeting.

"The district is trying to fire her," Salvador Salmon, Lori

Salmon's husband, told the reporters gathered outside the meeting room. "That's the reason we're trying to get the media involved."

When questioned by the media, school board members declined to comment because the matter was not officially before them.

"The community support really helped my client's case," Lawler said. "The community's feelings would have to be considered before the board took action. I think that the meeting gave district officials a reason to re-evaluate their stance."

Lawler used the community support at the school board to his advantage. The day after the meeting, Lawler requested a meeting with district officials to discuss the case and Superintendent Como granted the request.

The *Denver Post* ran its first story on the case on April 28, 2000. The story was a blurb in the "Western Empire" section. The paragraph-long story explained why Salmon was facing termination and that a meeting had been granted. Lawler was the only person quoted in the story.

"I'm surprised it has gotten to this point," Lawler told the reporter. "From her point of view, her actions were in the best interest of Michael."

Meetings and Momentum

The news articles and letters to the editor ceased during the months leading up to the meeting. The incident was slowly fading to the back of the public consciousness. Despite the lack of spotlight, the case was moving forward.

The evidentiary meeting began on June 15, 2000, with Superintendent Como, the school district's attorney, Salmon and Lawler. The district argued that Salmon's actions constituted a neglect of duty and abuse. The school district attorney indicated that he had interviewed Michael and Mr. and Mrs. Burn.

He claimed that the boy complained about the lack of heat, and the parents complained that they had not been informed before their child was placed in the room.

The school district's attorney then offered statements from Principal Pañera. The principal claimed that he had no knowledge of Salmon's use of the vestibule in the past. The principal maintained that he had not authorized her actions in Michael's case either.

Because he did not have written proof of Pañera's authorization, Lawler did not directly challenge the principal's version of events. Instead, Lawler introduced statements from Salmon and the other teachers who used the vestibule. By entering numerous witness statements from teachers who had also used the vestibule into the record, Lawler believed Superintendent Como would see through the principal's transparent story.

Lawler continued his arguments by introducing Salmon's grade book for the superintendent's review. He showed that Michael would have flunked because of all of his late and missing assignments. By showing Salmon's grade book before Michael's ten days in the vestibule and the grade book after Michael's time in the small room, Lawler successfully demonstrated that Salmon's method had caught Michael up with the rest of his classmates which would allow him to pass to the next grade.

Superintendent Como did not want to reinstate Salmon. He stated that he planned to ask the school board to terminate Salmon's contract. The school board was set to receive termination charges during their meeting that evening.

During the time between the meeting with Superintendent Como and the school board meeting, Lawler tried to reach a resolution to the case. Salmon was growing tired and frustrated and Lawler worried about the effects that a termination would have on her. To avoid subjecting Salmon to a public spectacle, Lawler asked Superintendent Como if they could make a deal.

"I was worried that if the school board terminated her contract, the negative publicity would ensure that my client never taught in the district again," Lawler said. "I was afraid the positive momentum we had gained through the media coverage would be lost if she was terminated. The public would be galvanized against her. In that political climate, even if she was successful in a termination hearing, the school board would terminate her anyway, as was the case with Al Wilder. The final meeting was a last ditch effort to avoid termination. In anticipating the need to put as much pressure on the school district as possible, I'd devised a nuclear fail-safe plan. Como never saw it coming.

"As we discussed a possible deal Como's jaw was set," Lawler said. "He was going to push ahead with the termination. He told me that there would be no negotiations."

Lawler had other ideas.

"I had my investigator look for written evidence of Principal Pañera's knowledge that the vestibule was being used to help catch students up. My investigator found a teacher who saved every e-mail she received. Two years before Salmon was suspended, Pañera had sent out a blanket e-mail discussing the ground rules for teachers who used the vestibule. My investigator asked her to print out a copy and she did. I had brought the documentation to the meeting but hadn't informed the school district that I had obtained them. I told Superintendent Como that I knew the school district supported the teacher's actions and that I could prove it," Lawler said.

Como was unmoved by Lawler's claim. Superintendent Como informed Lawler that he did not believe that the e-mails would carry enough wait to obtain a recommendation for retention in a termination hearing. Lawler smiled wolfishly.

"I don't plan to use them only in a termination hearing," Lawler said.

As he was replying to Como, Lawler walked to a window at the back of the room with a drawn shade. Lawler held the printed e-mails up where Como could see them and pulled up the shade. Outside, members of the media had their cameras with them, waiting for a statement from Lawler and Como.

"I told the media we were meeting today," Lawler said. "I have this memo and I'm sure that the media would love to read it. We can either work together, or I walk out there, hand the reporters my evidence and give the school district a black eye."

Como looked from the cameras to Lawler.

"Let's make a deal," Superintendent Como said.

The Aftermath

The next day, the *Denver Post* ran a story detailing the outcome of the negotiations. Salmon was reinstated, but she would be transferred to an alternative school where she would teach juvenile delinquents. She would also receive a reprimand in her file.

The article quoted Como as saying, "The school district determined that the jail school would be an appropriate position for her, and Ms. Salmon agreed. The school district decided that what it needed to do was assure students that this conduct would not be tolerated. I think we've done that."

Salmon started work at the school for juvenile delinquents the following week. She has been teaching there ever since. Salmon states that her job is more fulfilling than her previous position.

"She loves it," Lawler said. "She has a place in her heart for kids on the edge of dropping out. That's why she took such an interest in Michael. She wanted to help him. At her new school, she can dedicate her career to making sure all kids get a good education. It's a rare teacher that can do what she does."

Salmon's efforts with Michael did not make an impact because his parents saw an opportunity to profit from the case. They sued the school district and Salmon personally.

"The boy used the lawsuit as an excuse for his poor performance and never improved academically," Lawler said. "The parents traded dollars for their son's education which they must not have put a high value on. They settled for an amount that could only be described as nuisance pay."

Lawler believes the lawsuits and termination threats were unnecessary.

"The case was both simple and complex," Lawler said. "Because it was simple, it resolved itself. However, a lot of time was lost because the school district officials felt pressured to act by the media coverage the case received. I believe that without the media coverage, Salmon would have been returned to work within weeks of the complaint and the boy would not have missed out on an opportunity to better himself."

Chapter 13
Gus Ford

The Beginning

On May 1, 2002, Gus Ford gathered his old magazines and arranged them on the table in front of him. He opened the periodicals and began thumbing through them, looking for the perfect letters. When he found each desired letter, Ford cut it from the magazine and glued it to a piece of white typing paper. The work was tedious and time consuming, but Ford couldn't help smiling as he spelled out "The Flood has failed. You must die." Stephanie Kanon had been so uptight lately; Ford hoped his joke would help her relax.

Kanon taught the FLOOD program at Flat Irons Elementary School in Boulder, Colorado – a predominately affluent, Caucasian school. FLOOD was a literacy program designed to raise students' scores on the Colorado Student Assessment Exam – CSAP. The results from the most recent test had come back and FLOOD students had scored just under what school officials had expected of the program. After learning of her students' performance, Kanon had panicked. Kanon told Ford in a hushed voice that she believed the district would fire her for her student's performance or, worse yet, cancel the program.

Ford and Kanon had been friends for years. Despite Kanon's tightly wound persona and poor social skills, Ford found her to be an exceptional teacher. From experience, Ford knew that she would be asked to raise her students' performance, but the district would not punish Kanon or her program. Because the two joked with each other frequently, Ford hoped to assuage his colleague's fears with humor. The absurdity of a death threat over test scores would help Kanon regain a much-needed perspective about her students' test performance.

Ford finished the letter and sealed it in a plain white envelope and then went to bed for the night. The teacher planned the execution of his prank thoroughly. Kanon habitually did not pick up her school mail until noon, just as her lunch period was ending. During his lunch period, Ford went to the office and placed the envelope in Kanon's mailbox. He then slipped around the corner and waited for Kanon to appear. Ford wanted to jump out from his hiding place, just as Kanon read the prank letter.

He waited for almost twenty minutes. Ford kept checking his watch, afraid that he would be late for his next class. Ford had no way of knowing that Kanon had been delayed because she was talking to an administrator about one of her students. Ford was running out of time, and he needed to leave for class. As the bell rang for the next period to begin, Ford made a fateful decision. Kanon knew Ford was a prankster, and he assumed that she would know the letter was from him. Out of time, Ford had to leave for class. He planned to talk to Kanon after the last school period; he was sure they would have a good laugh over his joke.

The Complaint

Ford went back to his class and quickly forgot about the letter. He didn't think about his prank again until an announcement was broadcast over the school's intercom system. All faculty members were required to be at an emergency meeting following the last class of the school day. The message sounded ominous.

After the last class of the day, Ford went to the office to see if he could get some information about the meeting from one of the secretaries. He was friendly with the office assistants and they quickly filled him in on the reason behind the meeting. A teacher had received a death threat and the principal, Sandra Ayers, knew that it had to have come from within the school because there was no postmark on it.

Ford was embarrassed. His angular face flushed red, and he quickly ran his fingers through his thick brown hair, Ford immediately asked to see Principal Ayers and was led into her office.

"You know the meeting about the death threat?" Ford asked Ayers. "There's no need for it. I wrote it as a joke. Kanon is upset about the CSAP results, and I was trying to get her to lighten up."

"That was really stupid," Ayers said. "Stephanie Kanon is panicking. She thinks it is for real. I already called elementary Superintendent Nancy Ortega and she's going over the records of everyone who was in the office. We also notified the police."

"Is it too late to stop this?"

"Kanon went home because she was so upset. She lives down the street. Run over and apologize to her. We'll talk about how to resolve the rest of this situation when you get back. I know it was just a joke, but I may have to give you a reprimand."

Ford said he understood and ran from the school to Kanon's house. He made good time and was there within five minutes. Kanon's house was quiet. He rang the doorbell repeatedly, but no one answered. Although he wanted to talk with Kanon in person, Ford left a letter explaining the joke with an apology and returned to the school.

Ford made his way to the principal's office. Assistant Superintendent Ortega, a heavy-set Hispanic woman with short black hair, was seated in Ayers's office, waiting for him. Ortega's presence made Ford swallow hard. He'd had problems with the Assistant Superintendent in the past and he had now given her ammunition to get back at him. Ayers noticed Ford's discomfort and smiled at him. Feeling reassured, Ford explained to the women that Kanon wasn't at home, but that he had left a note on her door.

"I also left a message on her machine," Ayers said. "I'm sure that she'll be relieved to find out that it was just a joke."

"Do you need me to do anything else?" Ford asked.

"No. I'll start drafting your letter of reprimand. I'll have you sign it when I'm done."

Ortega sat listening to the entire conversation. At the mention of a reprimand, she sat forward quickly.

"I don't agree with that action," Ortega said to Ayers. "He made a death threat against a fellow teacher. We need to have the police investigate the incident. Following their investigation, I'm recommending the termination of his contract to the school board."

"That's a little too harsh," Ayers said. "Mr. Ford is an exceptional teacher who made a dumb mistake. I don't think he should be terminated for this."

Ortega shook her head and wagged her finger at Ayers.

"This was more than a dumb mistake," she said. "Mr. Ford is suspended with pay, pending district action."

Ortega then turned her attention to Ford.

"You have fifteen minutes to gather your belongings and vacate the building."

Ford quickly packed up his desk and exited the building. Because he had been suspended after the school day, he did not have a chance to say good-bye to his students. He went home and called the CEA.

The CEA Investigation

Greg Lawler was assigned to the case with another attorney. He immediately contracted with an investigator to begin looking into the incident.

Lawler then called the detectives assigned to the case to ascertain what charges would be filed.

"They were not pressing charges," Lawler said. "After talking to Principal Ayers, Kanon, and Ford, the investigators determined that no charges were warranted. It was just a case of bad judgment on Ford's part. The joke was ill-advised, but there was nothing criminal about it."

With the criminal aspect of the case resolved, Lawler focused on the repercussions to Ford's career. He started by calling the school district's attorney, Jason Foley, in order to work out a deal to avoid termination.

"Foley told me that the school district would not make a deal," Lawler said. "He explained that the district had a zero tolerance policy and that Ford could either resign or be terminated."

At the time, there were substantiated rumors that Principal Ayers did not want to terminate Ford. Instead, she wanted to give him a reprimand.

His students noticed Ford's absence from the classroom. Because Ford's suspension happened after school hours, the students did not know why he was being kept from them.

"I started getting calls from parents who wanted to know what was going on with their child's favorite teacher," Lawler said. "Everyone who called me claimed that the school officials were refusing to give them answers and they wanted to know what was happening. When I explained the reason for the suspension, they were incredulous. The parents kept telling me about what a great teacher and kind man Ford was. The parents said that it was obvious the death threat was a joke because Ford would not hurt anyone."

Lawler tried to speak with Kanon, but she refused on advice of school district counsel.

"It came out later that Kanon made the report because she didn't think that the death threat came from Ford," Lawler said. "She actually thought that it came from a second grade teacher who she had problems with. Once she realized that it was a joke, it was too late. She'd already made the report. The irony of the situation was that Ford was her only friend at the school. According to other teachers, Kanon did not get along with anyone at the school except Ford. Ford got along with everyone. If Ford had been there at the time she read the note, Kanon probably would not have filed charges."

The Media Coverage

The parents of students at Flat Irons Elementary School were outraged by the school district's disciplinary actions. Because of their business dealings, the parents had contacts with the local media. Independent of the CEA, the Flat Irons Elementary community launched their own publicity campaign.

The *Boulder Daily Camera* ran the first story on the incident on May 21, 2002. The story detailed the prank letter and the school district's reaction to it. The news article touched off a flood of letters to the editor. Ford's students and their parents wrote to the paper, begging for their teacher's immediate reinstatement.

Soon, Denver's major papers covered the story and carried news of Ford's suspension statewide. On May 27, the *Denver Rocky Mountain News* ran an article with the headline "*Students want teacher back; instructor put on leave for threat he says was a joke.*"

The article quoted a nine-year-old boy as saying, "Mr. Ford was the best teacher I've ever had. He plays with his students and is never mean. Please let him come back."

Along with the media pressure, the parents were actively appealing to the school board. Parents and students inundated the board with over two hundred letters from students and parents supporting Ford.

"The community was behind Ford," Lawler said. "Because of the public pressure, the media supported him, too. It was an odd case. In any other school, if a teacher had written a death threat letter, even jokingly, there would have been a mob demanding he lose his job. This situation was the opposite. Even the editorial pages were supporting Ford."

On May 30, the *Denver Rocky Mountain News* ran an editorial critical of the school district. The editorial was titled "*Idiotic Zero Tolerance, Again; The Issue: A teacher could lose their job over joke; Our view: It was a joke, not a threat.*"

The headline said it all. The newspaper writer stated that Ford had a third-grader's sense of humor and that if Ford was fired for his humor, any teacher was vulnerable to termination. According to the editorial writer, having a bad sense of humor wasn't a crime, but a necessity when dealing with young children. A third-grade sense of humor helps teachers relate to students. The editorial blasted the Boulder School District's "zero tolerance" policy and called Ford a valuable teaching asset.

Despite the massive media coverage, the school board was unmoved by the media attention and the public support that it generated for Ford. The school board, following the superintendent's recommendation, set a termination hearing for August 19, 2002.

"Despite the overwhelming public support for Ford, the school district wanted to terminate my client," Lawler said. "They were making an example of him."

Lawler tried again to reach a settlement in the case.

"They wouldn't budge," Lawler said. "I couldn't understand what their motivation was. The school district simply would not move to a middle ground regarding their efforts to discipline Ford. The superintendent wouldn't meet with us, and there was very little communication from them. It looked to me like the school district was hiding something or someone with a lot of authority who had a personal agenda."

Past History

Lawler turned to his investigator for the answers. Ford provided the investigator with his personal history of friction with Ortega, and the investigator used the past as a starting point. Within a few weeks, the investigator informed the attorneys that she'd found the source of Ortega's hard-line stance.

"Ortega had a past history with my client," Lawler explained. "She vehemently disliked Ford and wanted to see him terminated. I believe that the reasons for Ortega's actions were personally motivated by her issues with Ford and her struggles with the principal and parents of students at that school."

The source of the personal friction began nearly two years before Ford's joke gone awry.

The school's enrollment had declined rapidly. School district guidelines stipulated a specific student to teacher ratio. Because the ratio at Flat Irons Elementary had dropped, they had a surplus of one teacher. To comply with district guidelines, the school district needed to transfer a teacher to an understaffed school. School district policy dictated that the teacher with the least amount of seniority be transferred.

"The school district needed to reassign only one teacher," Lawler said. "The two teachers considered were Ford and Kanon. Ortega selected Ford for the transfer, but Principal Ayers and the parents at the school fought her. Ayers wanted Ford to stay because he was a great teacher. Ortega's decision to transfer Ford instead of Kanon disregarded Ayers's and the parents' wishes, and the parents at the school resented Ortega for that."

Flat Irons parents threatened Ortega to hold their kids out of school on count day, the day that the state counted student heads to determine the budget for the next school year.

"The parents probably wouldn't have held their kids out, but Ortega couldn't take that chance," Lawler said. "The loss of revenue would have been blamed on her, and that would have jeopardized her career. The move was a strong show of support for Ford. Ortega had ignored the parents before that point, but she couldn't dismiss them any longer."

Afraid that the parents would follow through with their plan, Ortega backed down. Neither Ford nor Kanon was transferred.

"The decision to leave the teaching staff intact was a compromise," Lawler explained. "To save face, Ortega offered any teacher in the school the chance to transfer voluntarily, and one teacher took her up on the offer."

Despite the personal victory, Ford would pay a heavy price for it.

"Ortega viewed that as a personal defeat," Lawler said. "She blamed Ford, and now she had an opportunity to get back at him. The prank was stupid on Ford's part. We've never argued any differently. Without the personal history, I think the entire incident would have ended with the apology and written reprimand."

While Lawler dealt with media requests and preparations for the hearing, he was working with the parents. Several of the parents had political contacts and had called their local senator. The senator offered to help. The senator contacted school board officials on behalf of the concerned parents.

"He was very vocal," Lawler said. "That was another difference in this case. I don't think very many teachers would have a senator come to their defense. That was a result of the parents' power and influence."

Ortega knew that community members were against her request for Ford's dismissal and took matters into her own hands. On June 15, 2002, Ortega held a meeting with the concerned parents.

"After that meeting, I got a lot of calls from worried parents," Lawler said. "At the meeting, Ortega told the gathering that if they knew everything that she did, they would thank her. Everyone wanted to know what I wasn't telling them. I reassured them that the CEA wasn't keeping anything from them, and that the reason for the disciplinary action was just what we said it was – the prank.

"The senator heard about Ortega's comments and also called me with concerns about Ortega's comments. If the senator got involved and it turned out Ford was not the moral man he had been made out to be, the senator would take a political hit. I had to explain that the comments were not valid, and that they were part of a negative publicity campaign by the school district. Finally, to reassure everyone, I released the recommendation to the school board that cited the prank as the only reason for termination. The

Boulder Daily Camera printed the entire document and everyone felt better."

After the parents of the school read the news article, they were frustrated because it appeared that school district officials had not been straightforward with them. They expressed their feelings through phone calls to school district officials and Ford's attorneys.

"They thought that they had been lied to, and they were angry," Lawler said. "The comments were meant to swing public support to the school district, but it backfired on them. Her misstatement made the parents even more determined to see Ford returned to the classroom. This case is important because it shows how legal issues can snowball into public relations nightmares. If Ford had been dealt with fairly from the beginning, the school district and Ford would have walked away with their respective reputations intact. Because the district chose to be adversarial, the parents witnessed an ugly spectacle."

Settlement

Lawler believed he had enough information to force a negotiation. While Superintendent James Crowder, Ortega's boss, refused to meet, he did agree to have Personnel Director Carla Lyel meet with the attorneys.

"We'd been asking for a meeting with Crowder throughout the entire process," Lawler said. "He kept refusing. Now, with the termination hearing drawing close, he agreed to have an underling talk to us."

Crowder's stand-in refused to negotiate at first, stating she was moving ahead with the termination. Frustrated, Lawler began laying out Ford's case against the school district.

"I went through everything point by point," Lawler said. "I gave her Ford's past history with Ortega, documentation on a racist comment made to Principal Ayers that may have contributed to Ortega's current actions and a statement from Kanon stating that the teacher did not want Ford terminated. Her eyes registered shock when I pulled out the documentation on the racist comment. I don't think she realized we had uncovered that information. As far as the school district was concerned, the incident was buried.

"Now, as she's taking a hard-line stance to support her administrator, we produced the records. It couldn't have been worse timing for them. The school district lost any advantage they had going into that meeting. I've often wondered if the reason Crowder put off meeting with us for so long was a hope that the incident would resolve itself and Ortega's comments wouldn't have to become public knowledge."

Lyel looked at Lawler for a second, and then she conceded, "We have a political problem."

The meeting concluded and Crowder began to negotiate with Lawler through his lawyer, but he refused to let Ford remain at Flat Irons.

"Ford got a reprimand in his personnel file," Lawler said. "The district was adamant that Ford be transferred. We argued that point for hours, but the district wouldn't back down. Eventually, we had to agree to those terms."

The Aftermath

Ford returned to the classroom for the 2002-2003 school year. Although he's at a different school, he is already enjoying enormous support from the parents there.

"The parents all realize he's an exceptional teacher," Lawler said. "He'll do well at any school. I'm not sure why the district wanted him transferred, but if it was to diminish his power by removing him from the parents at Flat Irons, they failed."

Kanon is still teaching at Flat Irons Elementary School. She is hoping that her FLOOD students improve dramatically over last year's CSAP results. She still argues that Ford's actions were well intended and that he did not deserve to be disciplined. Kanon does not hold any ill feelings towards Ford.

Lawler is bothered by the lack of discipline for Assistant Superintendent Ortega.

"To my knowledge she was never formally disciplined for her racist comments," Lawler said. "Had she been a white male, she would have been terminated and publicly branded a racist. As it stands now, she's not going to be held accountable for her racist words."

Chapter 14
Scott Rowland

The Beginning

    Brian Ringer pulled up the collar of his black raincoat as he stepped from the apartment building where his fellow gang member, Jason Brooks, lived. The massive black rain clouds, which blanketed Denver, blotted out the stars in the night sky. A strong gust of wind blew drops of rain into Ringer's face, and he quickly wiped them away. Through the torrent, he could see the cause of the loud bang that had summoned him from the cozy confines of his friend's apartment. A taxicab had smashed into the back of Brooks' large SUV.

    Brooks was already at his car, appraising the damage and yelling at the driver. Ringer sensed the presence of his two friends, Donald Pleasant and John Forrest as they joined him at Brooks' side.

    "Damn foreigner smashed Brooks' car," Forrest said to no one in particular. "Those people should go back where they came from. I bet he doesn't even speak English."

    The three men joined Brooks at the SUV. Even in the limited light, the three friends could see that Brooks' face was bright red. His friend gestured for the cab driver to get out of the car, but the small black man remained behind the wheel.

    Mustaffa Shariffe had been driving home after his shift. He'd hydroplaned over a puddle of water and skidded into the back of the SUV. A native of Morocco, Shariffe spoke only broken English. Shariffe sat petrified in his car with four large black men yelling at him in a language with which he was not completely familiar.

Brooks ordered Shariffe out of the car again, but the scared cab driver shook his head.

"I'll handle it," Ringer told Brooks.

Ringer walked up to the window of the cab and gestured for the cab driver to roll down the window. Shariffe, afraid to move, looked with wide eyes at the six-foot-four Ringer. A spark of anger flared deep inside Ringer. He thrust his arm back and slammed his elbow into the window. The window disintegrated into a shower of glass shards. Several of the shards cut Ringer and his anger swelled.

Ringer reached his hand through the glass and he grabbed Shariffe by the hair. Ringer pulled forcefully, yanking the cab driver through the window.

"You don't want to listen, we have ways of dealing with that," Ringer said.

Shariffe now stood with his back pressed against the cab. There was no escape. Ringer and his three friends formed a circle around Shariffe. Each of the men yelled and cursed at the frightened cab driver.

"What were you thinking?" Ringer yelled.

Shariffe could only mutter, "I'm sorry. I'm sorry."

"'Sorry' is not good enough," Ringer yelled. As he spoke, Ringer reared back his fist and slammed it forcefully into Shariffe's right temple. Shariffe stumbled backwards but stayed on his feet. Ringer swung again. This time, his fist connected with the cab driver's nose. Blood gushed, and Shariffe dropped to his knees. Ringer saw Shariffe's abdomen exposed and lashed out with his foot. Shariffe's body crumpled to the ground. Blood pooled under him before it was washed by the rainwater into red rivulets that flowed into the sewage gutter along the side of the street.

Ringer's three friends began to follow his lead. The three men pummeled Shariffe's body, exercising their anger on the unconscious cab driver. The young men began to lose energy within minutes, and the frenzied assault slowly ceased.

"Roll him over and wake his sorry ass up so I can get his insurance information," Brooks said.

Ringer bent over Shariffe's body, rolled him over and tried to make him sit up. The cab driver's head rolled backwards, unnaturally. For the first time, Ringer noticed that Shariffe was not breathing. Ringer checked him for a pulse, but found none.

"This guy is dead," Ringer said. "Doesn't matter though, he deserved it."

Ringer's three friends were not as calm. The three men began to panic. Ringer yelled at them to calm down and gave them instructions.

"Stuff his body in the trunk of his cab for tonight. We'll figure out what to do with the car in the morning."

Ringer's three friends complied. It took their combined efforts to lift Shariffe's corpse and place it in the trunk.

"Now let's go have a beer," Ringer said.

The three men started to walk back to the apartment when they heard police sirens.

"Shit," Ringer said. "One of the neighbors must have called the pigs. Run! If they catch you, remember they don't have anything on us. They can't prove we did anything unless we talk."

The four friends began to run from the police. Brooks was the slowest of the group. His three friends got away, but Brooks was caught. Cornered and scared, he gave the police permission to search his apartment.

Brooks did not know that in the time he had spent with the police, Ringer had run into the apartment and changed clothes. The police found Ringer's bloody clothes during their search.

The police then got a warrant to search the cab out front. There, they discovered Shariffe's pummeled corpse.

With the evidence against him mounting, Brooks rolled on his three friends. He described the fight in detail, focusing particularly on Ringer's actions.

The police called the coroner and took Brooks into custody. They also issued arrest warrants for Ringer and his two friends. Ringer was arrested two days later at his aunt's house.

Denver's newspapers covered the arrest of Ringer and his friends extensively. The first story ran in the *Denver Post* in April, 1998.

Scott Rowland, Ringer's former gym teacher at George Washington High School, sat in his real estate office reading the paper. When he saw the story about Ringer's arrest for murder, Rowland's blood went cold. The name Ringer could be common, and Rowland

---

hoped that he was mistaken. The former teacher hoped the murderer was not his former student, but when he saw Ringer's picture in the paper, Rowland had no doubt.

He would never forget the terrible look on Ringer's face as he beat a fellow student to within minutes of death. Rowland lit a cigarette and leaned back in his black leather chair. His mind was filled with questions. The most troubling question for Rowland was, "What if…?"

Rowland had prevented Ringer from killing a boy in 1996, and the actions the former teacher took that day had cost him his teaching career. Rowland wondered if the Denver Public School's administration had acted differently in 1996, would Shariffe still be alive? No matter what the answer was, the handling of the incident could only be described one way – as a missed opportunity.

History and Heroics

By 1996, Rowland had been teaching physical education for twenty years. He'd started at George Washington High School when the school had been filled with more affluent students. The school had changed over the years. Slowly, the area around George Washington had become part of the inner city. During the 1990s, the school was overrun with gangs. To enter the school, students and teachers had to pass through a metal detector.

Ringer had been in Rowland's gym class in 1996. The boy was a good athlete, but a dangerous person. Ringer's brother was a confirmed gang member, and Ringer had displayed violent tendencies, but the administration had never taken a firm disciplinary stance on either brother's actions. Students and faculty at the school had been afraid of Ringer and gave the boy a wide berth. The students that crossed him were beaten savagely.

In March, 1996, Rowland stayed late after school. He entered the gym on that fateful day to do paperwork. As he entered the gym, Rowland heard swearing and yelling mixed with pleas for help.

He tried to locate the source of the noise and pinpointed the location of the disturbance. It was coming from the end of a long row of bleachers. Ringer was straddled on top of a boy, hitting him mercilessly. Rowland yelled for Ringer to stop, but the boy did not respond.

Rowland rushed over to Ringer and tried to pull him off the boy, but Ringer was in a fit of rage and would not be stopped. Rowland looked for a way to stop the beating and saw a basketball against the far wall.

Rowland rushed over to the ball, picked it up and hurled it at Ringer. The ball found its mark and Ringer looked up with fury in his eyes. Ringer got up off the boy and started to walk menacingly towards Ringer.

"That's far enough," Rowland said.

Ringer kept coming, and Rowland had to shove him back.

As Ringer was about to swing, another teacher entered the room. The teacher got between Rowland and Ringer. Ringer seemed to calm down. With Ringer out of the way, Rowland rushed over to the semi-conscious boy Ringer had been beating and helped him to his feet. Rowland used his arm to steady the boy and walked him to the nurse's office while the other teacher walked Ringer to the principal's office.

Rowland thought the incident was over and went back to the gym to finish his paperwork. On the way there, Principal Sam Lewis stopped him.

Lewis asked Rowland to follow him to the office, and Rowland complied. Once there, Lewis informed Rowland that Ringer was making an accusation of abuse against Rowland and that the boy had bruises to back up his story.

Rowland gave Lewis his version of the events, expecting that the truth would end the matter.

"You hit him with a basketball?" Lewis asked.

Rowland agreed he had, but explained that he had to take the action to keep Ringer from killing the boy.

"Did you also shove him?"

"Yes. I was protecting myself."

"Ringer claims you were the aggressor and that he has witnesses."

"There was no one else in the gym."

"That's something we'll have to investigate. For now, I'm suspending you with pay and notifying the police."

Rowland went home and called the CEA. He didn't think he needed representation, but it never hurt to be prepared. In the end, he would be thankful that Greg Lawler was assigned as his counsel.

Lawler's Investigation

"After I talked to Rowland, I couldn't believe he was facing criminal charges and a possible termination," Lawler said. "Rowland should have been given a medal. He saved that boy's life. Since the school district had called the police, I needed to deal with any possible criminal charges before I could begin work on getting my client re-instated."

Lawler contracted the services of his investigator and called the City Attorneys' Office to find out what, if any, charges would be filed.

"The City Attorney's office was fairly adamant that criminal charges needed to be filed," Lawler said. "Ringer had gotten numerous students to back up his version of events. The police had witnesses stating that my client was the aggressor and that he didn't have to throw the basketball at Ringer. Because of the bruise on Ringer from where the ball struck him and the witness statements, the City Attorney was planning on filing assault and battery charges."

Formal criminal charges against Rowland were filed in early March, 1996. Because the offenses were misdemeanors, Rowland was not arrested. The case was set for trial during the first week of May.

"I had my investigator talk to the supposed witnesses. I also requested a full background check on Ringer," Lawler said. "Any kid with that much rage most likely had a past history of violent actions. If I could prove Ringer had a history of violence, I could establish that Ringer's actions that day fit with his history."

Lawler's investigator did not have to look very hard for the evidence needed. The investigator pulled Ringer's criminal history and civil lawsuits filed against him in the county.

"Ringer had been named in a wrongful death lawsuit in early 1996," Lawler said. "One man was wounded and another killed during a gun fight at the local Hyatt Regency Hotel. Ringer had a record of violence before the charges against Rowland were filed, and his pattern of abusive behavior continued afterward."

His neighbors had complained that he was selling drugs out of his apartment. In late March, 1996, Ringer was arrested for distributing cocaine.

On March 14, Ringer, Forrest and Brooks had attacked a man at the Hyatt Regency Hotel. Ringer apparently screamed his gang affiliation and threw hot coffee into the man's face. His two friends then proceeded to beat the man.

"A clear history of violence was established," Lawler said. "Not only could we prove that Ringer was the aggressor in Rowland's case, I could demonstrate that Ringer's violence was escalating. Instead of disciplining Rowland, the school should have been trying to help Ringer. The kid clearly had a problem. By getting Rowland into trouble, the school district was feeding Ringer's violent behavior patterns. They gave him a feeling of invincibility. Ringer must have felt like he could get away with anything."

With Ringer's history established, Lawler needed to uncover the reason that the witnesses in the case were lying.

"My investigator talked to the kids, and they were all telling the exact same story, which was a red flag," Lawler said. "The only person that could have influenced them was Ringer. I asked the investigator to interview them off school grounds, where Ringer would not be able to know that they had been interviewed. The move worked.

"Some of the kids kept their stories the same, but a few began to admit that they hadn't been there. The reason that they'd lied was that they were afraid of Ringer. He'd promised to do to them what he'd done to the boy in the gymnasium if they didn't go along with him. We turned that information over to the prosecutor, but that didn't change anything. They were going to trial."

The Trial

Rowland's trial started in May, 1996. Prosecutor Dan Wilkins opened the proceedings. Wilkins called Ringer to the stand. Ringer testified that he and the boy had stopped fighting and that Rowland had assaulted him. Ringer testified that he had not and would not ever do anything to harm the teacher.

"That testimony opened the door for me," Lawler said. "I couldn't introduce his prior bad acts except to impeach his testimony. I cross-examined him on all of his past incidents of violence. Ringer tried to wiggle out of it by saying that I was lying, but I had the legal documents from every incident. Eventually he had to admit that he had been violent in the past."

The prosecutor then called the witnesses who hadn't changed their stories. Each witness claimed that Rowland had been the aggressor.

"Under cross-examination, all but one admitted that they hadn't been in the gymnasium. They testified they had been pressured to lie by Ringer."

The prosecution rested its case, and Lawler began the defense.

"I called Rowland to the stand, and he gave his version of events. He described in explicit detail how Ringer was straddled on top of a helpless boy beating him senseless. Rowland described how he broke up the fight and how Ringer walked toward him threateningly. His testimony left little doubt in the juror's minds as to who the aggressor was, and nothing the prosecutor did could change that. The prosecutor cross-examined him, but my client's story was consistent and believable. He didn't poke any holes into Rowland's testimony."

Lawler then called the witnesses who had admitted that they had lied to the police.

"They each told varying accounts of how Ringer had threatened them," Lawler said. "I established that Ringer was lying, and his threats were the reasons that the case went to trial."

Lawler rested his case, and the trial moved to closing arguments. Closing arguments were concluded at four pm on May 8.

"It was so late in the day, I didn't think we'd get a verdict until the next afternoon. I was wrong. The jury came back within minutes. They'd found Rowland not guilty on all counts."

The Aftermath

Rowland was immediately reinstated. Despite having his name cleared, Rowland felt a deep anger.

"He saved a boy's life, and the school district rewarded him with a suspension," Lawler said. "I'd be angry as well. This was a case where the school district clearly needed to back up their employee. Rowland had a reasonable expectation that the school district would deal with him fairly, and instead they disciplined him. The district's actions ran counter to any type of logic."

Rowland quit his job and took the test for his real estate license. He has been working as a realtor ever since.

Ringer was never punished for making a false accusation against Rowland. His two-day suspension for fighting was the only disciplinary action he faced.

"He threatened his peers and beat a student senseless," Lawler said. "At the very least, he should have been suspended for a longer period of time.

"The school district had a chance to send Ringer and other students a clear message," Lawler said. "Instead they let him go. They had a chance to stop the boy's escalating violence but were too afraid of a civil suit to act. Instead, Ringer's violent behavior escalated until he finally murdered someone."

For his part in Shariffe's murder, Ringer received a life term at the Canyon City Correctional Facility. Ringer's aunt, Gretchen Malle, agreed to be interviewed after Ringer was sentenced.

"[Ringer] could not have committed a crime like that, never, ever in his life," Malle said. "They falsely accused him and it hurts. He's a beautiful person. That's God's child."

The family's comments did not surprise Lawler.

"From school officials to his family, everyone turned a blind eye to his escalating violence. The family has nothing left but denial. The truth of the situation is hard to face. If Ringer had been disciplined by the school and family earlier, Ringer's crimes might not have escalated to murder."

Chapter 15
Protecting Teachers

Overview

The thirteen cases examined in *Guilty Until Proven Innocent* have several things in common. Each case highlights a breakdown in the educational system, whether it was friction between teachers and administrators, poor investigative procedures, failure to properly discipline students for false allegations or an inability to defend teachers despite mounting evidence of innocence.

The cases also illuminate problems within the judicial and legislative systems. Falsely accused teachers face aggressive prosecution and legislation driven by public sentiment, limited legal options due to state statutes and unwillingness on the part of judges and prosecutors to believe teachers instead of students.

The problems faced by teachers in the cases examined are common. Because the standard taught to students – to report anything that makes them uncomfortable – is ambiguous, teachers can now be prosecuted or terminated for anything from language used in their lectures to intervening in a playground fight. The current reporting standard is extremely malleable, shaped by each individual student's life experiences and mental acuity. The broad nature of the uncomfortable standard directly affects the number of teachers falsely accused of abuse.

The majority of the cases documented in *Guilty Until Proven Innocent* were covered by the media, including the eventual revelations that the allegations were false, yet American society is still apt to believe that if a teacher is arrested, he must have done something wrong. Recently, the Colorado Legislature has been trying to codify that belief into law.

Currently, Colorado state law requires a teacher who is convicted of a felony be reported to the Colorado Department of Education. In 2003, the legislature began debate on House Bill 03-1176. The bill restricts teachers' right to due process. In Section Four, Part 2 the wording for the proposed amendment to the law states:

> Upon receiving notice from the Colorado Bureau of Investigation that a person who holds a license or authorization pursuant to the provisions of article 60.5 (teacher license) has been arrested for an offense specified in subsection 3 of this section (a misdemeanor or felony except for traffic offenses), the department shall immediately report such fact to the school district that is the current employer or the last known employer of the person.

"The CEA is vigorously fighting the proposed amendment. The proposed amendment underscores the message of this book that teachers accused of abuse are presumed guilty by the courts, media and the public," Lawler said. "The new amendment requires reporting any arrest for a misdemeanor offense. There is no due process; the accused teacher is immediately presumed guilty. An arrest or charge is not evidence of guilt. Despite the lack of legal weight an arrest carries, the legislature wants to use it as a standard to negatively affect teachers' careers. Certainly, the school district should be notified of alleged sexual offenses, but the legislature is categorizing all offenses with felony sex offenses.

"The fact that a misdemeanor offense can affect someone's career before there's been an investigation, court finding or an admission of guilt contradicts everything for which our society stands. American society is in danger of becoming the fascists Bertolucci warned us about in *1900*. This proposed law strips fundamental due process rights from teachers. At its core, the proposal is legislators placing a blind faith in the police to never arrest an innocent person. That faith is not supported by any fact based study or court.

"The framers of the Constitution built in judicial safeguards which the courts adhere to daily when cases are appealed because they recognized mistakes can and are made. Legislators are not trying to be unjust or evil by proposing this amendment, but they are reacting to a societal outcry. The proposed legislation is a reactionary, impulsive measure. Like anything done impulsively, the proposed law was not thought through very well."

HB-03-1176 seeks not only to force reports of misdemeanor arrests to the accused teacher's employer but also to limit the accused's legal defense options. In part, the proposed amendment to CRS 13-1-130 Reports of Convictions to Department of Education reads:

> When a person is convicted OF, pleads nolo contender To, or receives a deferred sentence OR DEFERRED PROSECUTION for a felony and the court knows the person is a current or former employee of a School District or charter school in this state or holds a license or authorization pursuant to the provisions of article 60.5, the court will report such fact to the department of education.

"The deferred prosecution amendment broadens the scope of an unjust law," Lawler explains. "A deferred prosecution is where the accused essentially pleads 'not guilty' and that is the only thing on record. The prosecution agrees that they will not press ahead with the charges provided the defendant does not have new charges leveled against them for a certain period of time. After a number of years, the entire incident is removed from the teacher's record. A deferred prosecution is where there's no conviction, so essentially, the teacher is deemed to have done nothing illegal. Despite the lack of evidence or a determination by a court, the legislature wants to change the plea to mean the same thing as a conviction. If the amendment passes, there's no due process and a teacher's only avenue to fight the charge will be a protracted court battle. Attorneys for the CEA used to only accept a dismissal of charges or a deferred prosecution. The plea is a way to save the courts, teacher and school district a lot of time, money and angst. They are rarely given except in cases where the District Attorney does not have a case. The plea is a manner of face-saving for the prosecution because prosecutors have the mindset that they would rather lose a case than out-and-out dismiss it. That's why the legislature created the plea; it's a benefit to the accused. Now the legislature is trying to take that option away. They are literally redefining a plea of innocence as an admission of guilt."

The legislature's activities coincide with Colorado Supreme Court cases that will profoundly affect educator's legal protections.

Keith Widder was a custodian in Durango, Colorado, who intervened to stop a bully from picking on another student. During the exchange, Widder and the bully's head accidentally bumped. The school district terminated Widder for the accident. Following the termination, Widder filed a lawsuit with the district court, using the Chapel Legislation and the Appeals Court's interpretation of the legislation in the Apple case. The district court found for Widder, but the school district appealed to the Colorado Court of Appeals. The appeals court ruled in the school district's favor and vacated the lower court's decision. In the process, the Colorado Court of Appeals rewrote the statute.

The Appeals Court ruling stated: "*Whom the School District Determines to Have Acted In Good Faith.*"

The wording change to the Chapel Legislation leaves school district's disciplinary actions unchecked. The change literally gives school districts the power to prosecute, judge and fact find against a teacher.

"The court changed the law fundamentally. It completely gutted it," Lawler said. "Now, school districts get to determine who acted in good faith in their duties. As the cases in *Guilty Until Proven Innocent* document, that's the equivalent of the fox guarding the hen house. Instead of a hearing in front of an impartial hearing officer, a school district can now hold its own hearing, never call a witness or present evidence, terminate the teacher and then say that the teacher was given a fair hearing."

The Colorado Supreme Court granted Widder's case Certiorari on October 18, 2002. The case will be decided in 2003.

"The public wants their children protected at all costs," Lawler said. "If the Chapel Legislation is nullified by the courts, many innocent teachers will be victimized by the legal system. If educators aren't free to go about their daily duties without fear of prosecution, discipline and safety will be further diminished with a detrimental result of diminished student learning. A lot is at stake with the Colorado Supreme Court ruling."

Public Misconceptions

School boards have the final say after they receive termination charges or hearing officer recommendations. Lawler believes that American courts' willingness to strip teachers of their constitutional rights is based in part on the public's belief that school boards are impartial arbiters of all educational matters.

"Society's general belief is that a teacher can appeal to a school board if they have been unjustly accused and that the matter will be dealt with fairly. That misconception highlights a myth about the educational legal process."

Lawler maintains that school boards can be prejudiced because their members are answerable to the public and are often prone to outside influences.

"The reality is that school board members are not necessarily impartial," Lawler said. "In most cases, each individual school board member has his own attorney. The attorney advises them on what to do. The attorneys have a great deal of influence over the school boards and they are not impartial.

"There are a few exceptions to the rule, but with all the lawsuits in today's society, school board members have to rely on their legal advisers to avoid being sued themselves. School board members are often reticent to replace the judgment of their legal counsels with their own judgement, because of the counsels' perceived specialized training and experience . Because the attorneys have relatively unchecked power over the boards, which can result in the persecution of innocent teachers, the public needs to realize that school boards do not balance the legal scales."

Media Misconceptions

School districts and school boards try to avoid publicity – especially negative publicity. Any time a teacher gets into trouble for any reason, the teacher becomes potential fodder for the media and a liability for the school district.

"Right or wrong, any professional who comes into daily contact with children, whether they be teachers, priests, counselors or day care workers, those professionals have a higher probability of becoming entangled in negative publicity than other professionals," Lawler said.

Priests and teachers have been on the two ends of the media spectrum. Teachers have had to deal openly with accusations of abuse and the legislative fall out for decades, where as the Catholic Church has only in the last few years begun to experience the probing nature of the press.

"The members of the press view the alleged crimes as a violation of trust and present the cases to the public from that perspective," Lawler said. "The coverage feeds the public's mistrust of teachers which causes members of society to want to limit the legal protections afforded teachers.

"Reporters are currently able to use dark quotes from unnamed sources, report the name of the accused and protect the privacy of the victim by withholding their name. The reporter is shielded from any errors by the First Amendment as long as the story was written in good faith. If a teacher is accused of a crime, there needs to be a level of privacy until a determination of the validity of the allegation can be made. I'm aware that American jurisprudence is based on an open court system, but limits have been in place for years, such as not allowing child victims' names to be revealed in the press, not allowing child victims to be photographed and limiting the media's access to the courtroom. A teacher can never regain their reputation under current reporting procedures because once accused, their reputation is permanently tarnished."

Jane Maxson, the vice-president for Teachers of the United School Employees of Pasco, Florida, points out that in order to make sure victims of abuse are not retraumatized, the media and the courts disguise their identity. This protection is meant as a shield, but when a false allegation is made, the protection becomes a sword. The accused is defenseless to keep his name and reputation from being soiled because the courts and the media report the accuser's name. This policy needs to be re-examined. Because of the rise in false allegations, the accused should be afforded anonymity until a determination or admission can be obtained. Without anonymity, the accused cannot return to normal life after his ordeal because of the societal stigma attached to him, even if he is found innocent of all wrongdoing.

"Those involved in working with children in the educational setting have genuine concerns relating to child abuse. They must deal with the total child. When the child arrives at school, he frequently brings additional baggage with him that affects all school employees. Examples of such baggage are neglect, mental abuse, physical abuse, sexual abuse and abuse by the child protective system. Therefore the laws designed to protect the child and provide him with the safest possible environment of necessity directly influence the educator," Maxson wrote.

Lawler maintains that anonymity for accused teachers will not place students in jeopardy. He states that the vast majority of abuse cases in Colorado are false allegations and that the few legitimate reports are driving the legislative process.

"There are a few cases that I've defended where the teacher actually committed the crime they were accused of," Lawler said. "It's the minority of cases that have a basis in fact that are causing problems. Similar to the few pedophile priests giving the Catholic Church a bad name, the teachers that commit crimes against students taint every teacher. Prior to the actions of the few bad teachers, there was no need for background checks or things of that nature. Now, teachers must pass a thorough background check before they can be employed."

Similar to the Puritans' view of Quakers as witches, teachers are seen by society as pedophiles until they prove that they are not. There is a growing perception by modern society that the teacher has done something wrong if charges are filed. In the absence of a change in the media's naming of accused abusers, the public needs to be conscious of the shortcomings of media reports. Relying only on media coverage to form an opinion of events is dangerous. The reality of a situation may be perceived differently than it actually existed because of the media outlet's need to generate ad revenue. Citizens should be encouraged to carefully consider what they read. Education in public schools and colleges, as well as discussion groups via the internet, can give citizens the tools necessary to scrutinize media reports.

Legislative Issues and Proposed Changes

"The current legislative movement is moving in the wrong direction; the pendulum has swung to strip teachers of their rights," Lawler said. "You cannot legislate a perfect teacher. As the cases documented in this book demonstrate, a myopic view opposed to putting the mistake in context of the overall career of the teacher warps the legislative efforts that limit teacher protections. I think that if the public reflects on their actions, they'll see that several protections need to be added, not taken away. The impetus for the changes is media reports that depict the problem of abuse as growing and widespread. Several studies, one of which was noted in the article "Violations of Trust", printed by the *Journal of Faculty Development* for the University of North Carolina, demonstrates that the problem of abuse is no more prevalent with teachers than with other trusted professionals."

One crucial protection to enact is mandatory accountability for adults or students who make false allegations.

"Students who make false allegations need to, at the very least, be suspended for the first offense and expelled for the second," Lawler said. "If we hold students accountable, the rate of false abuse reports across the nation will decline. The argument on the other side is that students will be afraid to make allegations of abuse. To counter that, I'd say that in order to suspend a student there needs to be clear evidence that the accusation of abuse was false. The change to the law has not been enacted or discussed for the simple reason that school boards fear civil lawsuits. This is an instance where the lawyers for school board members need to step out of the equation and let the school districts do the right thing."

Lawler maintains that along with greater accountability for students, there has to be increased scrutiny for the motives of adults and administrators when charges of abuse are leveled against an individual teacher. Lawler asserts that the tension between Joseph Anderson and his principal, documented in Chapter 1, contributed to the false allegations made against Anderson. According to Lawler, the Lisa Ridgeway case, documented in Chapter 2, is another example of friction between administrators and teachers giving rise to false allegations. Because of the variables that comprise an abuse allegation, several protective measures need to be taken to ensure that personal animosities are not leading to a false allegation. Among the protections are the following:

- Initial screening of the report by a neutral party to ascertain whether the facts are valid and verifiable.
- Thorough investigation of the allegations prior to criminal reporting or teacher suspension. Findings of the investigation should be made available to the accused teacher and their counsel.
- Accountability for staff members who make false allegations.

"The punishment for adults and administrators needs to be more severe than for students," Lawler said. "Suspension without pay or termination needs to result. Right now, adults can fabricate charges and get away with it. If we hold teachers accountable, it sends a message to students that no one is immune from the law. Adults know the consequences for their actions and need to be disciplined more forcefully because of that."

Along with greater accountability, Lawler would also like more openness in the investigative process.

"School's investigative records need to be made available to the defense," Lawler said. "If there are exculpatory statements in their investigation, the defense should be made aware of that. By opening the records, it lessens the chances of administrators pressing ahead with charges that they know to be false."

During a BBC News Conference held in Jersey, England, on April 18, 2001, Pat Lerew, Jules Donaldson and Tory Hague offered new insight into the problem of children falsely accusing educators of abuse.

Jules Donaldson stated, "Children must be listened to, allegations must be investigated, but children must not automatically be believed."

Another resolution to the increase in false allegations made against those in a position of trust is for parents to be made accountable for their children's behavior.

"If a child wrecks a phone box, the parents can be held responsible and made to pay for the damage. If a lying child wrecks someone's life there is no redress," said Pat Lerew.

William Hague also argued that anonymity be granted to the accused – as well as the accuser – until a determination has been made by a court.

The court system also must account for the erroneous, prejudicial reports when considering limiting teacher protections or prosecuting an accused abuser. Statistics kept by independent agencies show that a minority of educators and clergy abuse children. However, media reports have given the impression that the problem is reaching epidemic proportions. Judges are not immune to the societal debate, and the question of the media's impact on future judicial rulings and legislative actions must be elevated to an open national debate.

Higher Education

The changes and suggestions contained in this chapter are mainly aimed at helping teachers in the K-12 environment, but they can also be useful to college professors. Additional measures are needed to ensure that college professors are protected from false allegations. Legislative changes need to be made to allow state courts to intervene in college staffing issues.

The courts are not currently prohibited from this practice by legislative law. Instead, the barrier to has been set through prior court cases which established precedent. New laws would allow new precedent. A re-evaluation of current reporting policies to specifically protect professors' classroom speech is also needed.

Professors should be able to present subject matter without fear of termination. Specific legal language granting immunity for all reasonable speech necessary for academic discussion needs to be enacted.

Finally, an agency, independent of the college, should oversee disciplinary measures for sexual harassment complaints which stem from classroom lectures. Because of the litigious nature of society, colleges have adopted a zero-tolerance policy to stave off civil suits.

It is not currently in the college's best interest to defend professors accused of sexual harassment. It is cheaper to terminate the teacher and deal with any civil suit the professor might file. Because the college's neutrality is compromised by civil liability, the institution should not oversee both the investigation and the termination. An independent agency can speak with faculty and students to determine the exact nature of the comments and their relevance to the classroom setting.

"By working together with the many organizations having similar concerns, educators can educate their colleagues and others regarding the changes that need to happen – changes that will ensure everyone receives due process and that children are provided a safe atmosphere in which to learn," Maxson concludes. "A safe environment for the child is necessary, but it has to be accomplished without sacrificing the rights of innocent individuals. This great country was founded upon the principle of the presumption of innocence until proven guilty. Everyone must work together to guarantee this right to those falsely accused of child abuse."

Advice to Teachers

In the absence of laws protecting teachers, teachers need to take actions to protect themselves.

"The 'touchy feely' day when teachers could hug students is gone," Lawler said. "Some students need hugs for their self esteem, but teachers need to be careful. Often the most needy student is the most likely to make a false allegation of abuse. I'm not saying teachers should be robots, but before they hug a student, they need to think through the consequences. They all need to think about how they are going to hug the student and in what context the hug is given."

Teachers are most vulnerable to false allegations of abuse when they are placed in a one-on-one setting with a student.

"It's not always possible, but don't spend time with a student alone," Lawler said. "If they can, teachers need to make sure someone else is in the room. Another person present limits a student's ability to make a false allegation. If a teacher is alone with a student, leave the classroom door open."

In Jane Maxson's *Crisis of Trust*, the chilling impact of false allegations on educators is noted.

"School employees realize how vulnerable they are to being victims of false allegations by an unhappy student or parent," Maxson wrote. "Even when the report of suspected abuse is labeled as unfounded, they find their names have been entered into state registries.

"Teachers face hearings conducted by the state licensing boards and local school board. Those hearings are in addition to the child protective service, criminal, and possible civil hearings that occur when there has been an accusation of child abuse. As a result, many teachers have chosen to remove the nurturing touch in the classroom. Too many times the statement has been made, 'If we must err, let us err on the side of the child.' The present system is not erring on the side of the child. What happens to the lives of those individuals who have suffered because of these errors? Those teachers who have left the profession even after being cleared of all charges? The other teachers who have withdrawn from their students so that they will not suffer a similar fate? The guidance counselor or school nurse who is hesitant to see a child alone for fear of being falsely accused? The assistant superintendent of schools who committed suicide two days after a student recanted her story, but no one told him? The bus driver who spent three months in jail, suffered every imaginable indignity and a massive heart attack, later to be cleared? The school custodian who had charges dropped the day before trial by five girls who admitted they lied because he had reported them for vandalizing the restroom?"

Among Maxson's and the CEA's solutions to the problem which arise from false allegations of abuse is that teachers who work directly with children need to be included in discussions about restructuring the laws.

"If this is done, there could be an outstanding system that works for what is best for the child – a system that provides safety, a system that provides stability and emotional support, and a system that will benefit the child, the family, the educational system, and the nation," Maxson writes.

Students, teachers and administrators need to begin by developing a clear definition of child abuse and neglect. A clear definition will decrease confusion for mandated reports.

An additional change that should be explored is that of creating a purified child abuse registry. Unfounded and indicated charges should not appear in a registry. Teachers need to call their legislators and have input into the legislative process because what the legislature does affects their lives and careers.

To protect themselves, teachers also need to keep accurate records.

"If a teacher thinks something's weird or out of the ordinary, write down what happened and who was present," Lawler said. "If a teacher's actions get called into question, they already have the basis to assist their attorney in their investigation."

Lawler's last bit of advice to protect teachers from false allegations is to be alert.

"I've seen a lot of veteran teachers get accused of abuse," Lawler said. "What's happened is that they've become relaxed in the classroom and don't think through situations. Educators must always consider how a joke or a touch can be perceived if someone wants to twist it to their purposes."

If teachers follow those protections and still face allegations of abuse, Lawler advises them to say nothing.

"When an allegation is made against a teacher, that teacher needs to remain silent and retain counsel," Lawler suggests. "Often teachers know that they're innocent, and they want to clear their name. They try to explain their version of events to administrators, believing a simple explanation will end the issue. Their belief that a 'simple explanation' will suffice often exacerbates the situation. Everything they say can be twisted and used against them in later legal proceedings. Teachers must refuse to answer any questions or offer any explanation without an attorney present. If they are not represented by a union attorney, they should retain counsel. Once the allegation is made, the administrator the teacher is speaking to is no longer a friend or colleague. The relationship must be adversarial because the administrator needs to protect the school district. The administrator is no longer the teacher's ally.

"Also, teachers often don't get counsel because they think that they've done nothing wrong. They have faith that the system will deal with their situation fairly. Teachers falsely accused need to realize that they are assumed *Guilty Until Proven Innocent*. When they face allegations of abuse, administrators are not on the teachers' side. Falsely accused teachers want to believe the school district will protect them, but district officials have their own agenda. They're busy protecting themselves against civil suits. The school district will not believe a teacher is innocent because the allegation carries so much weight in society. Even if they've done nothing wrong, teachers should remain quiet and get an attorney. I can't emphasize that enough. When I say remain quiet, that means not talking to reporters. It's too easy for words to get twisted, slanted or manipulated to put the teacher in a bad light. I feel for teachers who have been wrongly accused, they want to clear their name, but talking to a reporter is not the way to do that. They should just get an attorney and let the attorney deal with the administration and the media."

Lawler believes the educational system is flawed as a result of the problems outlined in this book, but believes the remedies proposed in *Guilty Until Proven Innocent* will help repair the system.

"I'm not a fatalist," Lawler said. "There are a lot of good things about schools today. To be a strong society, we need well-educated citizenry. To have that, we need good teachers and when we get good teachers, we need to protect them.

"During the Salem Witch Trials, an individual would be ostracized by the population because of an allegation. To determine guilt, those accused often were cast into a river or pond. If the accused drowned, the public believed in their innocence; and, if the accused did not drown, they were assumed to be a witch. The phenomenon of abuse in schools mirrors that part of American history. Teachers' reputations and careers are being executed. To improve the educational system, protections to avoid drowning teachers in false allegations are needed."

12634490R00130

Made in the USA
Lexington, KY
19 December 2011